Stumbling Thru

Book One:
Hike Your Own Hike

Stumbling Thru

Book One:

Hike Your Own Hike

by

A. Digger Stolz

Follyworks Publishing, LLC
Copyright 2013

Published in the United States of America by
Follyworks Publishing, LLC.

Printed in the United States of America.

Library of Congress Control Number: 2013931771

Stolz, A. Digger
Stumbling Thru: Hike Your Own Hike: a novel / A. Digger Stolz
ISBN 978-0615763583

Follyworks Publishing, LLC, Niantic, Connecticut

First Edition

Book design by Stewart A. Williams

For Pops

One of the last things he said to me was, "Write your story."
And now I have.

Acknowledgements

I'd like to thank various and sundry people. Some for their help in bringing this project to fruition, some for their stalwart support over the past decades and some just because you never know when you're gonna get to write another acknowledgements page.

Bird—for being my wild muse and my wood nymph. For helping rehash and remember the golden days. For wanting to make a wall-sized chart showing where each character was at all times. The idea of that still gives me a migraine.

Mops—for letting me march to my own slow drum beat and supporting me no matter where in the world it took me.

B-Bop—for listening and reading and listening and reading and listening. Also, for that stash of Tooth Fairy money.

T-Ball—for holding my hand out there. I should've let you win a few games of cribbage.

Mr. & Mrs. Chauncey Chiasson—for a recuperative weekend away from trail way back when my feet were mincemeat.

Chicky Bird & Da Walrus—for the best trail magic of all: The Dirty Bird.

Bright-eyed Woodside—for covering all the angles: woman, thru-hiker, editor.

Hibs—for wanting to climb off Camel's Hump in the middle of a lightning storm.

Frizzle—for unwittingly packing a bottle of A1 Sauce eighteen miles.

C. Wall—for lots of good advice.

Ru-Dog—for all those pancakes at Sam's Sourdough Cafe.

The AT Crew—Captain, Load, Dirty Bird, Hutch, Ding, Skinny, Bandito, Sparrow, Frizzle, Spike, Pigeon Pot Pie, Lonestar and Old Man Chronic for talking the talks and walking the miles with me.

The AK Crew—Dr. Dickie Carr, Lanky Franky, Ken Lamerling, Shitcan, El Hefe, Marie D, Paddy Mac, My Crony, the Closet Kid and all the rest who made my transition from corporate butt-plug to learned man of letters as ~~educational~~ entertaining as possible.

Finally, a special thanks to every trail maintainer, volunteer, park ranger, hostelier, trail angel and anyone else who's had a role in making the Appalachian Trail experience what it is today: simply awesome.

A Note from the Author

First off, there is no one "right" way to thru-hike the Appalachian Trail.

Let's just put that out there.

And if I had to guess, I'd say there are roughly as many different ways to hike as there are people who have given thru-hiking the old college try.

So by no means do I intend to imply that some or any of my characters thru-hike the "right" way. If there is a "right" way (see line 1) I don't know it. Honestly, I don't even know a "good" way to thru-hike. All I know is my way. And my way isn't your way (see line 4).

All that being said, my intentions with this novel couldn't have been simpler. Firstly, I hoped to depict thru-hiking in such a way that everyone (armchair hikers, fuzzy-nutted rookies and crusty triple-crowners) could recognize and appreciate its special vibe. In that regard, I'll let you be the judge of my success. I don't remotely consider myself inspirational, but if there was a second intention, it was to motivate readers to climb a mountain, to hike their own hike, to unplug from the smartphone/laptop/joystick/remote and make time to get out on America's first and foremost National Scenic Trail. Or for that matter, any trail anywhere.

If you spend enough time on the AT, you will start to feel ownership. It's as inevitable as that burn in your thighs when climbing steeply uphill. But that's okay, because ownership is a good thing. It means people care. And when people care they donate time and money, they work to keep trails clear and clean, they strive to make the AT a better place. They also know enough about hiking, gear, trail locations and lore to quibble.

So allow me to apologize in advance. My descriptions may not do justice to your personal favorite mountaintop or a shelter/hostel/trail town you remember fondly. I may have gotten the mileage wrong somewhere. Or neglected to mention something you believe to be a quintessential aspect of the experience. If you feel ownership over the AT, I'm sure my descriptions *will* fail you at some point. More than once probably. It doesn't make me happy, but it does bring up an important point.

I thru-hiked in 1999. Since then, I've revisited lots and lots of the AT. This includes the seven hundred mile stretch between Amicalola and Pearisburg in 2011 and dozens of weekend/section hikes in the New England states. But things change. Fresh trail goes in, rotten shelters come out. Businesses come and go. New trail angels, icons and personalities pop up as old ones drop into the Great Hiker Box in the Ground. If my description of a place doesn't wholly jibe with your memories from a 1981 or 2005 thru-hike, consider that I might be describing trail as it was in 1999 or 2011 or maybe I'm taking some poetic license. Of course, it's also possible that I've simply screwed the pooch and gotten it wrong. For which I'm apologizing now.

It has taken me three abandoned attempts and more than a dozen years to get this novel working the way I dreamed. I spent hundreds of pages and many hours trying to force the story into a shape it didn't want to take before finally understanding my real goal: showcase the Appalachian Trail in all her glory. Somehow I needed to organically portray the ins and outs, the minutia, the mindsets and the gloriously grubby texture that is the thru-hiking experience. Of course, this meant not just using the trail as the scenic backdrop for a murder mystery or some other dynamic bit of genre fiction. Consequently, the following pages contain far too many characters and not nearly enough conflict. Be warned, this book features inane repetitions of the four inanely repetitious trail activities (walking/talking/eating/sleeping) and damn little else. This, I fully understand, does not make for active characters or a thrilling story, but it is an accurate representation of life on the Appalachian Trail.

It's essential that any realistic portrayal of the AT capture all the ridiculousness that takes place out there. For me, the primary trail reality is that thru-hiking can become monotonous. And monotony quickly becomes boring. But I don't mean to imply that boring is bad. Boring is the beginning. Boring is a welcome mat. Boring is what has to happen just before all the really good stuff goes down. Boring is why hikers come up with ridiculous games and partake in bizarre conversations; it's why one of my trail colleagues stole a three foot tall bar trophy on a bet, and another had to carry it up to the summit of Katahdin.

So with this new approach securely in mind, I trashed all my old pages and set about creating thousands of fresh trail moments, hundreds of hikers, at least a dozen story arcs, and one (mostly) linear timeline. All so I could show the AT the way I've seen her: nonsensically whimsical, ruthlessly challenging, tangentially fragmented, ceaselessly surprising, and altogether mysterious in a "you better believe Mother Nature knows best" kind of way.

In keeping with the "true" representation of the trail, I chose not to divvy Stumbling Thru into traditional chapter-sized blocks. Instead, I opted to capture micro-sections, small moments and quick snippets. I did this because it's how I remember time on the AT. When I reminisce with my old roll dogs from '99, we say things like "what about that long hitch we got with that family with the two screaming babies and one threw up on you" and "do you remember that time at Newfound Gap with the whiskey and the sword?" or "how 'bout that drunk dude in Duncannon who let us borrow his truck to get groceries?"

Our storytelling isn't linear. We don't recall what happened fifteen minutes to either side of the events in question. I can't hazard a guess as to why I was in a pub at 10:30 on the morning in question (other than the obvious reason). I can't remember who actually drove the drunk dude's truck but I do remember him saying, "Here, y'all can take my keys" just before underhand-lobbing them into the left breast of one of the female hikers in our crew. He did it nice and gentle, like he was tossing dimes at a carnival booth.

Squish. Clunk.

I remember all us guys sharing a look, wondering if we should be offended and rise up to defend our comrade's left breast or just take the keys, jam nine hikers into the drunk dude's pickup and make tracks for the nearest grocery store.

Being appropriately ravenous thru-hikers, we opted for the

groceries and bought the drunk dude a beer when we got back.

As you read, you may find scenes you believe aren't realistic. You *know* this couldn't happen or that creature wouldn't act a certain way. To that, let me say this. I am not a scientist, a zookeeper, a meteorologist, a botanist or any other kind of person with a degree that would imply they know something about something. My educational background implies I don't know anything much about anything except what I've seen with my own eyes. As a hard and fast rule, the more outlandish a scene seems to you, the closer it is to being based on actual, honest-to-God-I-did-it-saw-it-lived-it-myself reality. Snow can fall in Tennessee and the rattlesnake scene went down pretty much as I wrote it. Seriously. No kidding. Unbelievable, right?

I'd like to wind up by saying thanks to all the people who've had a hand in making the Appalachian Trail what it is today. I speak for more than myself when I say your toil is greatly appreciated.

Digger Stolz
January 2013

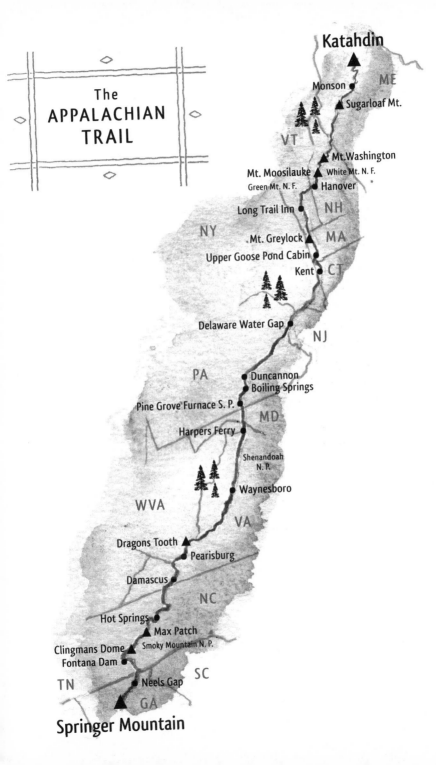

The
**APPALACHIAN
TRAIL**

Katahdin

Monson

Sugarloaf Mt.

ME

VT

Mt. Washington

Mt. Moosilauke   White Mt. N. F.

Green Mt. N. F.   Hanover

Long Trail Inn

NH

NY

Mt. Greylock   MA

Upper Goose Pond Cabin

Kent   CT

Delaware Water Gap

NJ

PA

Duncannon

Boiling Springs

Pine Grove Furnace S. P.

Harpers Ferry   MD

Shenandoah
N. P.

Waynesboro

WVA

VA

Dragons Tooth

Pearisburg

Damascus

NC

Hot Springs

Max Patch

Clingmans Dome   Smoky Mountain N. P.

Fontana Dam

TN   Neels Gap

SC

GA

Springer Mountain

PART ONE:

HIKE YOUR OWN HIKE

Nothing.

Walter felt nothing.

Which, honestly, was probably for the best. If he had felt something, he would've felt dredged out, empty and confused.

From the Visitor Center, he walked to the base of the falls. It was the simplest of strolls; a few hundred feet along a level, paved pathway. Unaccustomed as he was to the pressing weight of his backpack, it felt far longer.

The dark waters of Amicalola Falls crashed down and kicked up spray that was a hell of a lot colder than Walter would have ever guessed for early April in Georgia. Somewhere far above, the top of the falls was out of sight. A nearby staircase twined up and up like a sort of easy-access beanstalk for the modern day Jacks of this world. Sturdy wooden handrails and non-slip metal treads. Six-hundred steps, if he could believe the signs. He didn't bother to count.

Walter's legs were long enough to comfortably take the stairs two at a time. After the first dozen steps, he down-shifted to one stair per step. Already, there was an uncomfortable burning in his thighs.

At a hundred steps he was sweating. And not just at his brow. Armpits, chest, his whole face was wet.

At two-hundred he was wheezing and red-faced. Coughing some and rasping for air. He could feel the straps of his pack cutting into his shoulders, restricting blood flow. The pack's hipbelt was riding high, too close to his ribs and constricting his diaphragm, making it hard to catch a full breath.

At three-hundred steps Walter's entire body was huffing and puffing, squishing and squelching something fierce. It was a genuine racket, a cacophony of effort and moist output.

By the four-hundredth step, he could barely keep upright. He clutched at the handrail; his legs trembled like a newborn fawn's. He plomped down right there on the steps. With his backpack still on, he had to sit backwards, looking down at where he'd come from and pretty much plugging up the whole works.

After a bit, another hiker, a woman wearing a backpack less than half the size of his, climbed toward him. Walter watched her progressing along, rising with all the easy grace of a butterfly riding an updraft.

She was maybe just over the line into her thirties. Slight of frame, might've looked wispy, but for the strength of her stride as she climbed.

"Hey," she said. With a pointed nose over a bright smile, she wasn't beautiful, but he didn't want to take his eyes off her. There was something about her, something immediately appealing.

"Unh."

"You thru-hiking?"

He tried to shrug, but with his shoulders restrained by the pack straps, the gesture was mostly unsuccessful.

She wiped a hand against what looked like a dry brow, "Already sweating up a storm. Guess I'd better get used to it, right?"

3

He nodded, feeling it unnecessary to point out the dampness visibly soaking through his jeans and his favorite flannel shirt.

She stood there for a long awkward moment before he realized he was blocking the best part of the stairway.

"Sorry," he mumbled, heaving himself unsteadily upright, "figured you could just sort of...flutter by."

She giggled at that, but the sound was washed away with the roaring of the falls.

He shifted aside and sucked it all in, but still she had to brush against him as she passed. He smelled something then, a single citrus-y whiff of warmth and rolling meadows.

"Alright, well, see ya," she called back. A silky blonde pony-tail bobbed along in her wake. She disappeared round a bend in the staircase before he could blink.

At five-hundred steps or thereabouts, he leaned over the rail and spit up. Mostly it was bile and saliva and maybe just a little bit of the ham sandwich he'd eaten late last night.

At the top of the falls, Walter flopped to the ground in a tangle of numb limbs. Drooling a little, breathing a lot. Eyes closed, ears full of a roaring seashell noise. Wondering if this *adventure* of Angie's was going to kill him. Was maybe intended to kill him.

"Hey, Mister," a child's voice followed closely by a jab in the stomach.

"Is he dead?" a second child said.

"Still kinda moving."

"Looks dead."

Walter opened his eyes. A woman, presumably their mother, called the children away. He spit and groaned his way upright.

A car drove past. There was a road, paved and well-traveled not six feet from where he'd collapsed. Nearby, tourists were climbing down off a short tour bus and snapping pictures from the top of the falls. Across the road, a pickup stopped long enough for a tall guy and a short, chubby girl to clamber out of the back.

"Thanks. Saved us from climbing those stairs," the girl laughed. She tucked a wide-brimmed straw hat over pig-tails, shouldered a pack and set off up the trail. Bouncing with excitement and out of sight in no time. Easy as anything.

❦

After the nearly infinite stairs up the practically vertical waterfall, the trail gentled out to become a wide sandy footpath. Walter's boots scuffed along as the trail unfurled before him. He passed under towering pines whose burnt-orange needles gave the forest a certain soft-bedded hush. Slanting sunlight hinted at the season's coming warmth. Rhododendrons twisted in arched tunnels over the trail. Their flat, waxy leaves making cool shade. Overhead, yellow leaf buds freckled the highest tree and the first spray of wild flowers colored the ground. A single winged silhouette circled through the cloudless afternoon; the sole spectator to Walter's solitude.

Nice as all of it was, Walter could only shamble along like one of Romero's old school zombies. Those kids had it right, he was more dead than alive. It wasn't any sort of pretty. He wheezed, stumbled and stopped a lot. It was during those first painful miles that Walter came to understand some things about the pack on his back.

It was a big bastard: sixty-five pounds of canned beans, t-shirts, old sneakers and whatever else Angie had stuffed into it. A shoulder-pinching, back-snapping, soul-crushing sea anchor, a constant and considerable sap on his forward momentum. It was a drag, both literally and figuratively. She had borrowed it, along with some other bits of gear, from her nephew Tommy and promptly stuffed it beyond full with whatever came to mind. Extra tube socks, old paperbacks, a new roll of duct tape, spare D cell batteries for the flashlight, shampoo, a sloshing pink bottle of pepto and a tin of bandages. A tight foil packet of homemade sugar cookies. What didn't fit inside was tucked into outer pockets or strapped to the exterior. A sleeping pad, metal canteen, aluminum skillet, and finally an old yellow raincoat. Walter hadn't helped, but he'd sat nearby, watching in silence as she jammed and crammed and finally towards the end, got one of her legs up and actually stomped more and more down the pack's dark throat.

The rig wasn't simply heavy, a dead weight to be hefted and quietly lugged along. No, at times it seemed combatively alive, like an unwilling child being carried off to bed. A malevolent force for pain and discomfort, liable to pinch or chafe or throw its improperly secured load front-to-back or side-to-side with no warning and less sympathy. Too-tight shoulder straps hampered circulation, turned his hands a throbbing red. And the top lid towered precariously up above Walter's head, like the tumbling curl on a cresting wave.

❦ ❦ ❦

When Walter made the summit of Springer, the sun was a

great orange five-ball sinking into a deep and distant pocket over the green felt of Georgian hills. In the fading light, he nearly missed the bronze plaque. It was greened over and set into a low, flat rock face. Unbuckling his pack, he slumped down and watched the last cusp of sun drop out of sight.

Springer Mountain—the southern terminus, the official starting point of the Appalachian Trail. Tracing fingers over the plaque bestowed Walter with a vaguely hollow feeling, an unpleasant sensation of finality. Somehow, in the cool metal and raised lettering, he found tangible proof that these last hours, weeks and months of his life had all been starkly real. They weren't some bad dream or even symptoms of an actual straightforward problem that could be managed away or solved outright. This realization came hand in hand with a mental fatigue that far outweighed the physical exhaustion of his body.

With one last effort, Walter levered himself back to his feet. A wooden sign on a nearby tree pointed off to the right, towards Springer Mountain Shelter. He made his way silently, palely, mechanically; dragging his pack along behind as if it were wheeled luggage. It gouged a deep furrow in the dirt. The trail sloped down past an outhouse and finally to the packed dirt space around the shelter itself.

By now it was full on night. He couldn't see much beyond the glow of a campfire and the handful of shapes hunched around it. Laughter and low conversation faded away as he drew near.

The man-sized shape closest to Walter jerked in surprise and cried, "Jesus H. Chr—" before falling backwards off his log seat and exposing a jiggling-soft stomach and a vast waistline.

A brown fedora, stiff-brimmed and fresh-out-the-box crisp, went tumbling off his head.

"Scared the hell out of me," he gruffed, equal parts embarrassed and annoyed. Took some doing, but the big man found his feet, brushed the hat clean and lovingly resettled it in place. His tone softened when he got his first good look at Walter in the firelight.

"Christ a' mighty, son, you okay?"

Walter nodded unconvincingly.

"Well here, take a seat. Looks like you could sit for a bit."

Walter sat.

"My name's Stray Dog," the man gestured around the fire at the others, "and this here's Crumbs and Monterey Jack."

"Do not," Jack growled, "call me Monterey Jack. Already told you, I am not taking that name. No way, hombre."

Across the fire, Walter couldn't make out much more than tortoiseshell glasses setting off a cherubically chubby face.

"But it's perfect," Stray Dog said, "I mean, you're from Chicago and your initials would be MJ, like Michael Jordan. And, and you really did polish off that block of cheese earlier—"

"No deal. No dice."

"Or we could call you Jack Black. You're sort of shaped like—"

"Drop it or I start calling you Windy Indy," Jack countered, his voice sharp with inflection. "And I'll make it stick too."

Crumbs snickered, gave Walter a welcome nod, and kept on with fingering at his smartphone.

Stray Dog started up as if someone had asked him about his hiking plans, "So, I'm going all the way to Maine. Been a dream of mine since reading Bryson's *A Walk in the Woods*. Ever read it?

You should, it's good. Real good. Funniest book ever."

Jack made a muted gagging noise.

Stray Dog gave him a look, but kept on talking, "That Bryson is a funny guy. Got it with me, you want to borrow it. But anyway, I quit my job to come out here—life is just too damn short to spend it leashed to a desk. Planning to summit September first. My birthday. Gonna be sixty-three."

If Walter were inclined to converse, he hadn't the energy for it. Was all he could do to recline back against his pack, slip into a fire-induced trance and give off a vague impression of wakefulness.

Luckily, Stray Dog wasn't a needful man. Wasn't a traditionalist insisting that a conversation involve two or more active participants. He steamed right along, unaccompanied, as it were. Give the man a grunt or a distracted nod once every ten minutes and he might just go on 'til the apocalypse.

"Real name's Joe Everett. Stray Dog's my trail name You know that saying—'If you're not the lead dog, the scenery never changes'? Well, I spent the last thirty-nine years selling ad space for newspapers—couple different papers, few different markets. The scenery hadn't really changed a once in all those years. Always knew I wasn't the lead dog or nothing, but when I first realized I'd been staring straight up into the corporate, ah...."

"Butthole?" Jack offered.

Stray Dog nodded appreciatively, he hadn't wanted to say it. "And I realized how tired I was of it all. So that's when I decided to *stray* way from the pack, you know? Set off on my own and beat a new trail. Enough is enough, already, right?"

There was a rehearsed quality, a practiced rhythm to Stray

Dog's little freedom speech. Like maybe he'd spent some time polishing it. Convincing himself or loved ones that quitting his job and disappearing into the woods was really the only sensible option for him.

"So then I had to sell my wife on this idea. Easier than you—"

"I like it," Jack interrupted, "and I get it. Except, I don't really think of stray dogs as following any trail, you know? They stray *off* the beaten path. Find their own way. What you've gone and done is just trade one path for another. Corporate career path for an Appalachian footpath. Thousands of people come out here to hike every year, so at best you've only just joined a new pack. So I tell you what—I'm gonna respect the spirit of your name without actually, you know, using it."

"How's that now?"

"Gonna whittle it down, keep the S and T from stray, the D from dog. Call you STD instead."

"Er...that's not...."

A log popped, sent up a shower of sparks, cut off any argument from STD.

"But don't let me interrupt, seriously—you were saying about your wife?"

"Ah...yeah...well, at first, she was dead-set against it, but after thinking the whole thing through, she agreed a little time in the woods was exactly what I needed. Thought she wouldn't want to stay home by herself, you know, lonely, scared or whatever, but I swear she started looking forward to it. Made me sell my fishing boat—Stratos 186 XT, had this dandy one-seven-five Evinrude on back. A *real* beaut. Like to cry when she disappeared down the road. Dearly loved that boat, but I guess a little compromise is probably good for the soul—"

Crumbs glanced up from his phone, rolled his eyes and went right back to texting. He asked, "Where'd that blonde chick go?" without looking up again.

"Who, Flutterby? She disappeared off to her hammock." Jack leered, "Why do you care? Thought you were fluriously sexting with your girl."

"Fluriously isn't a word."

"Sure it is. Combination of furious and flurry. Made it up myself. Even submitted it to the Portmanteau Association of Oxford for recognition. Could hear back any day now."

Despite this side conversation, STD plowed on like an old farmer in his field, "—once the wife said yes, I had about a thousand things to do. Got onto a training regimen—walked four miles a day, five days a week at an indoor track. Even dropped a few pounds. Started pulling my gear kit together, studying up on that White Blazes website, seeing what I needed, what I didn't. Collected old boxes to put maildrops in. Sent them all out day before last—thirty-four boxes of supplies. Took me six trips into the post office. The counter lady made me promise to send her postcards, except she called them progress reports.

"Been talking this trip up for months now. They threw me a retirement party at work, everybody chipped in and got me hiking poles. Super lightweight carbonite; top of the line. Got my church praying for me every Sunday, too. Pretty much told everyone I knew I was goin' hiking. That's how I said it too, 'goin' hiking'. Yep—friends, family, even the UPS driver. I was his best customer all winter, what with all the gear and food and whatever else I been ordering for the trip. Delivered this hat too. Nice, right?"

STD offered the hat around. Nobody took it.

"It's wool felt with a grosgrain bow; brown on brown with a pinched crown. Cost three-hundred dollars, but I guess if you wanna go on an adventure, you'd better have yourself a good traveling hat.

"So here we are, Georgia to Maine on the Appalachian Trail. Do or die, you know? I'm getting to Katahdin or y'all are carrying me off trail in a pine box."

"That would be one big box."

Ignoring Jack, STD waved a hand around, "Isn't it amazing? Finally getting out here is like, I don't know, a dozen dreams all coming true at exactly the same moment. The peace and quiet, the rightness of the natural world all around us. Getting back to what matters. A thousand stars sparkling overhead. Rocks and roots beneath our feet. Nature's very own building blocks. Surrounded by great people. Am I right? Crumbs and Black Jack and—"

"I'm not taking that name," Jack growled.

Pointing to include Walter, STD continued, "—all of you. Y'all are great, just great."

STD stood up, scanned for firewood. "Gotta feed the fire, but before I do, let's put it on the record—all y'all are officially invited to climb Katahdin with me on my birthday. Mark your calendars. Won't that be something? What do you say?"

Crumbs' face tilted up from his phone long enough to express confusion.

"What day is that again? The first of September?" Jack paged through his mental calendar, "Yeah, that'd be okay—no wait, shit, you know what? I think—I do, I have a funeral that day. What're the odds, right? Sucks!"

As STD disappeared off into the darkness, Jack slugged off of a soda bottle, made a pained face. He passed the bottle to Crumbs who shot a quick mouthful and passed it back.

"Hey. Better have some, buddy," Jack whispered. "Sure makes Joey Fedora a whole lot easier to stomach and no offense, but you look pretty wrung out."

Walter took the bottle. Sniffed, shrugged, tilted it back. A firestorm went tumbling down his throat. Somehow he kept most of it down. Coughed, drooled, spat and gasped.

Finally, "What *was* that?"

Jack laughed hard, "Terrible, right? Guy who shuttled me from the airport, claimed to have a grandfather with a still. Big city mouse like me, I couldn't say no. Moonshine, turpentine, maybe rubbing alcohol, I don't know, but it's lighting me *up* inside."

STD returned with an armload of sticks, took his time feeding them to the fire. "Can't believe we're all sitting round a campfire up top of Springer," he said. "Reminds me of this one time I was camping back home in Indiana. See there was—"

The big man unleashed upon them a rambling, unflappably slow narrative told in the best Midwestern-style. That is, entirely without any regard for relevancy or audience interest but with a dogged belief that the story must continue on and on and on. It was generously sprinkled with unrelated anecdotes, distant cousins and a nonlinear chronicling of STD's formative youth.

Jack took up the shelter register, an old spiral-bound notebook, leaned close to the fire and perused it with an intensity that could've only been feigned. The register's front cover was dominated by a block-letter commandment:

HIKE
YOUR
OWN
HIKE!!!

While his smartphone battery held out, Crumbs kept himself digitally sequestered within the phone's electronic universe. Walter leaned back, resting against the bulk of his backpack, and simply let STD's words wash him away to a better time and place.

Walter woke fully clothed and shivering. His Morton Fisherman raincoat was tucked up to his chin. Stray embers had burnt more than a dozen little black holes into the legs of his jeans. His feet throbbed inside his boots. He was dry-mouthed and sniffly-nosed. Hungry. Headachy. Sore-necked and stiff-legged. About as disoriented and uncomfortable as a waking body gets. He was real slow in collecting his bearings; this partly due to a crazy striped wool hat snuggled down tight over his ears and eyes. Standing up was one man-sized, full body twinge of pain.

By the fresh light of the dawn, Walter got his first good look at the shelter. A post and beam superstructure resting on a foundation of six concrete piers. Weathered board and batten siding closed in three of the shelter's sides. The fourth side was open to the elements. Had a crumbly little stone patio, a raised floor and a high saltbox roof covered over with wooden shingles. The whole thing was relatively newish, or at least looked good for its age, but still the words rustic and rudimentary came springing straight to mind.

Walter could see that the height of the roof helped to give the place an open, well-lit feel. With no windows and something like a twelve by twelve footprint, open and well-lit were crucial qualities. Far as he understood, shelters were intended as hubs for humanity in the wilderness, gathering places for knowledge sharing and community and as fine refuges from rough weather. But for all that, if this one was a fair representation, they weren't any sort of place Walter wanted to spend the next however many months of his life.

Behind him, Walter heard the spring-slap of an outhouse door whinging closed.

He turned to see Jack walking back to the shelter, a roll of toilet paper tucked under one arm. In the morning light, Jack looked to be teddy bear soft and packed full of stuffing. Dark wispy hair was kept parted to one side, combed over and left long and straight in the back.

"Still alive?" Jack called. "We tried waking you, but you were dead to the world. Snoring so loud, you even drowned out STD after a while."

He retrieved the hat from Walter's hand. "Figured you'd get pretty cold when the fire died down." Jack shouldered his pack and headed off, "Guess I'll see you up the way."

Walter nodded, stumbled over, took a seat at the edge of the shelter. He sat there alone, suddenly aware of chirping birds and frantic chipmunks racing from tree to tree. Best as he could, he processed this improbable moment in his life. When the task proved unwelcome, he thumbed through the shelter notebook.

Register: Springer Mountain Shelter

3/19 Yesterday the movers came, packed everything up & drove it away. Sonny lives in a boring sub-division in Bismarck and says I'm too old to live by myself. Phooey! I showed him: I'm officially on the lam! Sent him a postcard from Amicalola. Poor kid's going to have a fit when he finds out. Here begins my best & last adventure!

The Knitty Biddy

Most of STD's first northbound mile on the Appalachian Trail was unqualified bliss. He started off hot-footing towards Maine first thing in the morning. Literally skipping along, propelled by exhilaration, enthusiasm and also gravity, as that first section of trail sloped gently downhill.

Along the path, white blazes were sporadically visible on trailside trees, marking the way. Proverbial breadcrumbs for lost children to find their way through an otherwise dark and tangled wood. That first mile, STD's heart fluttered each time a blaze appeared around the bend or over the next rise in the trail. Coming out of the gate, he'd actually kissed the first white blaze he passed.

It was good times and happy days. He breathed deep, filled his lungs with mountain air. The stuff was crisp and cool, fresh from the heavens above.

Similarly, the second mile passed by. And the third.

The fourth mile...not so much.

Somewhere in there, his feet started to hurt. Cured and stitched leather rubbed up against soft skin. Friction. Hotspots. Little baby blisters in waiting. White blossoms of pain and pus.

And everything was going slower than he'd been expecting. Thought he'd have covered twice the distance in the same time. And despite all the research and work he'd done to buy the lightest gear, carry only the absolute necessities—his pack still felt heavy. He'd been out walking all winter—five, sometimes six mornings a week at an indoor track, clocked a quick four miles each session. Course, that had been wearing sneakers and no pack over perfectly flat terrain. Passed pretty much everyone out there, except those young women who walked with a scowling determination and a pissed-off pace that generally had them lapping him. It was a little annoying but mostly okay, because it was nice watching them pass by. Just like that Flutterby. A good name too, one look at her and his heart took to fluttering. If he were a young man, well, he wasn't and anyway all that walking had been good exercise, sure, but now he realized it wasn't any sort of realistic preparation for thru-hiking. He was humping forty-odd pounds of gear up and down and up and down and up and down, and watching his footing every single step of the way. His back throbbed and his legs were half numb. Each one of his ten toes jammed into the front of his boots on the downhills. Heels rubbed and calves burned on the uphills.

By mile five, the trail was nothing like he'd expected it to be.

❦ ❦ ❦

Jack came up on STD a couple miles short of Hawk Mountain. STD was sitting on a trailside log patching over the worst of his blisters with moleskin.

"Those new boots?"

"Yup."

"Looks like they're getting you good, huh?"

"Yup."

"Staying at Hawk Mountain Shelter?"

"Nah. Wrap these feet up and shuffle on to Justus Creek."

"Should stay at Hawk Mountain. Ease into all this."

"Can't. Got a schedule. Sure not gonna make Maine by easing along."

❦ ❦ ❦

Flutterby settled into a strong pace. Which didn't surprise her much; she'd gotten out for a run every day over the last eighteen months. Passed STD and then a while later, that Crumbs kid. Some other people too. Got to Hawk Mountain Shelter a little after midday. First one there. Picnic table, fire ring, privy on the right, a little spring down a ways on the left. Place looked nice. All clean and clear with plenty of room for tenting. She stretched her hammock between two pines. The picnic table was half in shade, half out. She took a seat on the shady side, set to work on a bagel globbed high with peanut butter and dripping honey. Sat there eating mostly with her right hand which was a bit of a challenge. As much as was possible, she kept her left hand basking in direct sunlight. There was a band of pale skin on her ring finger that she was interested in tanning away as quickly as possible.

Lunch turned out to be a nice, peaceful moment to herself, which was exactly what Flutterby didn't need. These last months, she'd had more than her share of peaceful moments alone. When the moment was over, she went to hang her food bag on the bear cables beyond the shelter. These were half-inch metal cables looped up over pulleys suspended between two high trees. The process was simple: hook a food bag on one end of a cable and pull on the other end. When the food bag was swinging at least fifteen feet into the air (out of reach of even the biggest, cleverest bears), fasten the cable to a designated hook on a nearby tree.

From where she stood beneath the cables, Flutterby could just see the privy's corrugated roof. There still wasn't any rush in that department, but she couldn't put it off forever. Figured with no one around, this was as good a time as any to suffer through that particular indignity.

The privy building was about what she expected. The entrance was a swinging saloon door with no obvious locking mechanism; the stall walls consisted of three feet of plywood starting a foot from the floor. Apparently, privacy wasn't a high priority. Both the feet and head of a standing adult would be plainly visible from outside. The heads and shoulders of those souls braving contact with the seat would be just down out of view. The particularly tall and anyone thinking to hover instead of sit would look like a prairie dog to those queued up outside, waiting their turn.

Inside, the toilet base was bolted to a plywood floor. A simple white metal cylinder topped by a horseshoe-shaped seat. The place stunk bad, but that was something she knew all about. She'd spent the last eight years working as an ER nurse at an inner city hospital.

When Flutterby took a seat, she was immediately surrounded and strafed by buzzing flies, hordes of the little nasties—landing on her arms, walking across her forehead, flying up through her legs from below. And it didn't take a genius to guess what they'd last landed on. "Don't you dare look down there," she said to herself, "you'll end this whole thing before you've had a chance to start it."

She didn't look, but from the literature posted on the privy walls she came to understand it wasn't just a dank, dark hole down there. It was her distinct privilege to be making a deposit in a "moldering" privy. Moldering being a slow composting process in which human waste was dried out and decomposed with the help of oxygen and a bulking agent (bark and wood shavings). She was just getting to the part about how you weren't supposed to pee in the privy (oops) when she heard something. A metallic clinking noise. The shuffling bustle of large bodies.

Too big to be squirrels or some other little mammal monkeying around on the bear cables. Except for the metallic clinking it might've been a larger animal, a deer or even a bear trundling past.

Flutterby sat there still and quiet as an old stone. As the noise persisted, she worked her nerve up and peered over the privy wall. Not thirty feet away, a ragged line of men were walking past. They wore dark camouflage, combat boots and duck-billed caps. Some had face paint and most carried black rifles. They looked beaten down and near to broken. Shuffling, slumping, staggering along under full loads of weapons and ammunition, canteens, radios, bed rolls and whatever else it was they'd stuffed into their massive packs. Two soldiers carried a third between them, laid out in a stretcher. A few looked to have their eyes closed, even as they clumped along. One had tears streaming down dirty cheeks. Some didn't register her presence, though most went by with heads cocked, taking in the slender feet and the shorts down around slim ankles. To a man, they didn't say a word, not to her, not to one another.

❦ ❦ ❦

Register: Hawk Mountain Shelter

4/5   Took the midnight train
       to Georgia. Northward bound
       and feeling just peachy
                        High-Ku

❦ ❦ ❦

Walter's back ached, armpits and nethers chafed, head thumped and his pack still wobbled around like a wounded animal. With each plodding, trodding step thunderous booms of pain blossomed up from his feet. Walter was aware of these discomforts and more, but only vaguely so, as if he were detached and looking down on himself remotely. He didn't feel them so much as recognize each from a distance.

If nothing else, though, he had forward momentum. Wasn't gonna break any land-speed records, but considering his pack and all the physical griefs he was butting up against, it was a respectable distance for the second day. More than.

Which isn't to say no one overtook him. Seemed to be just about every shape and size hiker zipped past, kicked up dusty wakes and showed him their backsides.

It was late afternoon when Walter finally arrived at Hawk Mountain Shelter. He recognized many of the occupants. Most had passed him earlier in the day. A few old guys, a couple of women, the rest mostly kids in their twenties.

Walter squeezed into a spot at the picnic table. He sat there listening to various conversations. There was lots of tentative joking, bantering about pack weights, ounces shaved and gear carried.

Seemed like anyone with significant hiking experience trumpeted it for all to hear. A pony-tailed kid going by Hungry Joe had hiked the Colorado Trail. One high-cheeked woman spent three weeks on the Pacific Crest Trail. There was a bony thin man with a neatly trimmed beard and a quiet voice. He was on his sixth try at thru-hiking the AT. Called himself Again. Kept getting hurt or otherwise losing steam and having to go off trail, only to try it all *again* the next spring. Was happy to dispense advice but everyone flat ignored him. Who wanted hiking tips from a guy who couldn't make it to Maine in five tries?

Fritz was this blonde giant of a farm boy by way of the Black Forest. It took about seven seconds for someone to first call him Blitz. His shorts and shirt were unflattering in their Euro-tightness, his hands the size of frisbees and his appetite was endless. He cooked up and tossed down two heaping pots of noodles and still had room to help Flutterby with the last of her couscous pilaf.

Another hiker, Crazy Ray (this was more a description than an official trail name) hitched his way down to Georgia from way up in Vermont's Northeast Kingdom. He spoke with an accent that straddled the Canadian/American border and took the worst from both worlds. Had a sense of personal space that was eight inches shy of comfortable. Talking with him was a disconcerting, face-wiping affair. Crazy Ray chose not to carry any food. Instead, he opted to pack a Nerf football-sized stash of marijuana and planned to barter his way northward. So far he'd been eating like a king.

The Wabash Cannonball was fresh out of college and a colossal dud. When he wasn't all emo and teary-eyed, staring at a wallet-sized picture of his girlfriend, he was asking everyone what they missed most from back home.

Next to Walter, STD was worrying over his bare feet, dabbing Neosporin on hot spots. He had a blister bubble around back on his heel. Despite Again's advice that he leave it alone, STD popped the bubble and drained the pus. But couldn't quite see to clean or wrap the wound, so he'd wrangled Jack's help.

"Clean it out good. Poor some water on it or something, you know? Don't want any infections setting in on the first day."

"Don't worry." Jack winked at Walter and pulled out the soda bottle from the previous night. An inch or two of moonshine still sloshed at the bottom. "This might sting a little, STD."

"Don't worry about that, just make sure you get it good and cleaAAAAAAAA! What in Sam Hill was *that*?!?"

"You said water or something. It was something called moonshine. Want more?"

"No! No more!"

"You sure, man? It'll kill any germs you got."

"Hurts worse than that damn blister did."

Walter worked the laces of his boots free, pried a foot out. The sock was soaked through, equal parts sweat and blood and pus. It stuck to his foot, was a real bitch shucking it free. Had to ease it over his heel and roll it down the length of his foot.

"Holy *dogshit*, dude," Jack said.

The foot looked like uncooked meat. Not so much hamburg, as there was entirely a different texture to it, but more marbled and smooth, like a roast. Raw abrasions, blistery welts and open sores delineated rare patches of zombified skin—puckery, cold and white—where the boot hadn't yet gnawed at his foot.

A crowd gathered, gawped down at the disaster that was Walter's bare foot.

"You walked here, man?"

"Look at that."

"*That's* sick."

"*I'm* gonna be sick—"

"You're crazy." This from Crazy Ray.

"It's okay, everything's fine, you all can go back to your jerky," Jack announced to the crowd, "I'm a doctor." He bent down and looked closely at the foot, "And the doctor says," he swished the moonshine and grimaced, "you're going to need some big medicine."

With Jack's help, Walter removed the boot and sock from his other foot. It was just as grisly as the first.

STD studied Walter's boots, "Are these steel-toed? What—are you hoping to pick up a little construction work along the way?"

Jack nodded, "Got anything else to wear? Crocs, Tevas?"

"Sneakers."

"You're packing sneakers? Well, good—I guess. Try them tomorrow. Should be gentler going. Dump these big yellow bastards in the first garbage you find. Okay, now, take a big swig," Jack handed the bottle over. "This is gonna feel like I'm holding your feet to the fire."

Walter swallowed a mouthful before Jack dribbled the remaining moonshine over his feet. As the liquid splashed down, Jack cringed, expecting a pained outcry from his patient.

Walter might've gritted his teeth, but otherwise didn't show any reaction to Jack's big medicine.

"Zowie, man, you're one tough bastard, huh? Walk your feet down to bloody nubs and then you don't flinch when I douse them with what's probably pure alcohol."

Walter shrugged, "Not feeling so much of anything these days, you know?"

Best as he could without getting blood on his hands, Jack squirted Neosporin on both feet. "Here, rub that in. You got some fresh fucking socks? When you're done smearing that shit all around, put them on." Using a stick, he carried Walter's old socks to the campfire and dropped socks and stick into the flames.

✤

Like a favorite hoody, a comfortable darkness settled over the Georgian woods. Most everyone had disappeared into tents or slipped into sleeping bags laid out on the shelter floor.

It was just Walter and Jack left awake, both watching the campfire's last licks while companionably listening to the sounds of the night. A soothing blend of thrumming field crickets, rattling katydids and the high-pitched pulsing of Spring peepers. Nature's own evening sonata.

Walter worked his way through a cold can of baked beans. He'd tried cooking the beans by placing them on hot coals at the fire's edge, but that didn't do much more than burn the paper label off.

A small black notebook sat open on Jack's lap. He seemed expectant, poised to write, but pen and notebook hadn't yet been introduced. After about twenty minutes of painstaking consideration, Jack closed the notebook, tucked it away with a sigh and began sifting through a baggie of assorted pills. Had some trouble seeing what was what by the fire's dim glow. Eventually he located and popped a few "Perks." Pocketed an Ambien for later.

"You want an oxy or anything?" he whispered.

Walter shook his head, "So what kind of doctor are you?"

Jack chortled, "Well, I guess you could say I'm a doctor of

doublespeak and master of the intellectually irrelevant." He grinned, "Otherwise known as a Ph.D. in Literary Criticism. University of Chicago. Sartre and Derrida and fucking Chucky Baudelaire. Just defended my thesis a month ago. And before you even ask—it is just the most recent in a long line of ridiculous degrees that haven't prepared me to do one single useful thing out in the real world. Other than, you know, sling bullshit and talk in circles. Certainly nothing that might be conceived as meaningful or socially significant. Somewhere along the way, I also wrangled an M.S. in Psychology, an M.A. in Shakespearian Lit. and an M.F.A in Poetry. So yeah, it's official—I am over-fucking-educated and un-fucking-employable."

Walter almost chuckled, "Fucking bawdy."

"You're familiar with Baudelaire's work?"

"Was talking about you."

"Bawdy, huh?"

"Uh-huh."

"That's a pretty good goddamn trail name," Jack nodded appreciatively. "Yep. I think I'll take that one."

❧ ❧ ❧

Register: Gooch Mountain Shelter

4/2 You know you're in trouble when your hiking partner shows up in loafers.   —The Galloping Goose

❧ ❧ ❧

Half a mile short of Woody Gap. STD was limping along behind Walter stumping along behind a waddling Bawdy. The trail wound upwards towards Ramrock Mountain. A rocky outcrop near the summit provided a wide view out across the valley and back onto the AT itself. Or at least it did on clear days. This was not a clear day. Since mid-morning, dark clouds had been tumbling in from the east. Visibility was hovering just shy of twenty feet.

"Can't see shit," Bawdy said, as he dropped his pack and took a seat with his legs dangling over the rock ledge. He set to work on a tube of Pringles. Walter plopped down nearby, started making a sandwich: peanut butter on ridiculously smushed and already stale Wonder Bread.

"What'd you expect? Gonna start raining any time now, *Bawdy*," STD grumbled. He'd been in a mood pretty much since pulling his boots on that morning. Ten miles of hiking had done nothing to improve it. Neither had the news of Bawdy's new trail name.

"We gotta be close to Woody Gap now. Catch a hitch into Suches if you're afraid of melting, STD. Far as I can tell, you ain't nowhere near sweet enough for that though," Bawdy said.

"I'm not going to any damn hostel, hotel or anything else. Got ground to make up. Only the second day and I'm already behind schedule."

"Guess you gotta hike your own hike, man, but this *is* supposed to be enjoyable."

"Shame it's so goddamned slow going then." STD lurched off ahead.

Walter and Bawdy watched him disappear up trail.

"How's the feet?"

"Sneakers help," Walter managed through a mouthful of peanut butter. They sat there staring into the low cloud cover. At times it wafted past so close, it was like you could reach out and catch yourself a wisp.

"So, I got to admit, I'm curious as cat piss, Walter—whatever made you want to come out here? Doesn't really seem like any of this is your thing."

"Isn't," was his mildly cadaverous reply.

"Soooo?"

A long pause. "My wife drove me down to Amicalola. Dumped me off."

"I don't understand."

"I don't either." A longer pause. "She said this could be good for me—fresh air, exercise, a whole new perspective on things."

"And?"

Walter shrugged, "I said, 'I don't want to' and she said I pretty much had to or...you know."

Bawdy's look said he did not know.

"Or don't bother coming home. And I said, 'I really don't want to.' And then she left me standing in the parking lot."

Bawdy gaped, "You're joking?"

Walter shook his head.

"That's just like *Bartleby the Scrivener*."

"Yeah? What's that?"

"A short story by Melville. It's assigned reading for pretty much every college freshman in America these days."

Walter shrugged noncommittally.

"Old Bartleby was this scrivener dude, you know, like a

29

human Xerox, way back in the day. Was majorly depressed: overwhelmed by ennui or whatever. Whenever his boss asked him to do anything, his response was, 'I would prefer not to.' Got so he didn't do nothing but stand in a corner. That's a... that pretty much sounds like you, huh?"

❦

A guy appeared out of the mist. Ambling southward, steady and real slow. He was spindly thin, grayed over and weather-worn. Like how teak patio furniture gets after being left out-side for a few winters. Had a big Jeremiah Johnson beard going on. His boots scraped at the ground with every step. Generally carried himself like he was an old jalopy, beat to shit and running on empty.

He pulled up in the middle of trail, "I'm the Southbound Pachyderm, but mostly people call me Packy."

Just having gotten moving again, Bawdy didn't want to stop, but Packy was blocking trail.

"Hey there, Packy."

"You fellas thru-hiking?"

"We're giving it the old college try," Bawdy said. "Little early to say for sure."

"What're your names?"

"I'm Bawdy and I guess," he jerked a thumb back at Walter, "this is Bartleby. You coming all the way from Maine?"

"Left Katahdin on June 21st. Been cold, wet or hungry ever since. 'Cept for the bugs and the mice, I been alone out here since October. Took six weeks off for the holidays, and still had to snowshoe over the Smokies."

Packy sniffled. There was a crusty buildup of old snot on his mustache. "Toughest trip I ever took. Worst one too. Wish I never started the dang thing."

"Least you're almost done, huh?"

"Y'all should quit," Packy nodded, "before the hike gets into your blood. It's like a virus—once you got it, there ain't no cure. Can't do nuffin' but keep on keepin' on."

"Okay, then," Bawdy said. He started forward, edging around the southbounder.

"Best stop while you still can." There was something of a basset hound in Packy's sad-eyed countenance. He slowly wagged his head side to side, "Leastways, the big guy with the funny hat listened to me."

At Woody Gap the AT crossed its first paved road. GA-60. The rain started just as they rolled into the clearing.

Bawdy quick pointed at a car just pulling out of the parking lot. "Look. See that?"

Bartleby grunted interrogatively.

"That green Subaru. I swear STD was sitting in the passenger seat. Can't miss that stupid hat of his. He must've took a hitch. Weird, though. I think Suches is the other direction."

Bawdy and Bartleby stood in the beginnings of a cold rain and watched the Subaru disappear down around the bend. Bawdy shivered, picked up a pair of hiking poles left leaning against a picnic table. "These are his poles, aren't they? Big dope left them."

He tossed them to Bartleby, "Yours now."

"What do I do with them?"

"Hold on to them 'til he catches up. Like he said, they're

top of the line, probably cost more than all your gear combined. We leave them here, they'll disappear."

"You could—" Bartleby's protest died off. Bawdy already had his own pair of hiking poles.

❦ ❦ ❦

STD sat there in the passenger seat of a Subaru Outback. He was heading home. Or at least heading towards home via the closest bus station. And some to-be-determined number of stops along the way back to Indianapolis.

Stared out the window, couldn't help but wonder at how much faster things moved in the real world. It had only been a few days, but life in the woods was only as quick as your own feet. And it had turned out his feet weren't very quick and they hurt like hell and this whole thing hadn't been anything like it was supposed to be. With that goddamned kid calling him STD and the rain, he was glad he was quitting now, before it got into his blood.

❦ ❦ ❦

The trail rose sharply up and away from the gap. Bawdy and Bartleby slogged onward and upward for a few miles, but really, between the slippery footing, sodden clothes and cold water dribbling down their backs, it wasn't any kind of fun.

When they came up on Dan Gap, Bawdy took a studiously long look at his AT guidebook. Sussed out some options for the night. The nearest shelter was Woods Hole. It was five miles north and then a half-mile off trail to the west. Instead of racking up non-AT mileage, it made about as much sense to push another 1.3 miles beyond Woods Hole to Blood Mountain Shelter. Except that Blood Mountain Shelter was up on top of Blood Mountain, which looked to be a fifteen hundred foot elevation gain. And, being on a mountaintop, the shelter didn't have a reliable water source. So if he wanted to sleep under a roof tonight he was looking at hiking more than six miles, climbing fifteen hundred feet while packing water from the next stream he passed. And of course, that plan was entirely predicated on there still being room left in the shelter. Bawdy'd already come to the conclusion that, when you needed them most, shelters would have an annoying tendency to be fully occupied.

Ahead on the right, there was a flattish area big enough for a couple of tents. This was probably as good a spot as he was going to find.

"Guess I'm gonna set up here," Bawdy said. "You with me or what?"

Bartleby stood there blinking rain out of his eyes. He could have been calculating algorithms or sound asleep behind those open, empty eyes. Bawdy wouldn't have comfortably bet it either way.

When Bartleby nodded, Bawdy grinned. He'd spent the last thirty-six years living the soft life of a city mouse. He'd never spent a night alone in the woods. While he figured it would happen sometime during the next few months, he was happy to put it off as long as possible.

Before too long, he got his tarp stretched out and secured. Had a rectangular section of tyvek, a papery-thin construction material, for a ground cloth beneath his silnylon rip-stop tarp.

The stuff was light as air, but it crinkled something crazy. Bawdy went and filled his water bladder and one of Bartleby's bottles at a nearby stream. Took what he hoped was the last whiz of the night, stripped down and hung his wet t-shirt, shorts and skivvies on a nearby branch and crawled under the tarp.

After squirming into dry thermals and fleece socks, Bawdy set out a dog-eared copy of *Slaughterhouse-Five* so he could read himself to sleep. Pocketed an Ambien, just in case Vonnegut didn't deliver him to the Land of Nod. These chores accomplished, he fired up his homemade soda-can alcohol stove and put a pot on to boil. While that was happening, he sat and watched Bartleby monkey with his tent. It quickly became obvious the poor slob had less than no clue how to set the thing up.

"That goes in the back," Bawdy called. "No, the other piece. The one in your left hand. Now it's in your right hand. That. Yes. The back side of the tent. The other side is the back side."

Wife dumped him off at Amicalola. Was he kidding about that? Zowie—what a trip. Literally cast off to fend for himself in the Appalachian mountains. See you in a couple thousand miles, honey. Or not. That woman must be crazy as a bag-lady or absolutely desperate. This wasn't nothing like sleeping out in the backyard for a night.

That stupid yellow raincoat had to weigh four pounds alone. To say nothing about Bartleby's work boots—hard to imagine walking even a single mile in them or on those beat to hell feet of his.

"There ya go. Got it now," Bawdy called. "Nice work."

Bartleby stood back for a moment to appreciate his handiwork.

No matter how he arranged the stakes, shifted the poles or tightened guy lines, he couldn't quite eliminate a curious swaybacked sag that ran along the tent's ridgeline. Sort of looked like he might be missing a piece or two.

The tent was up. Its effectiveness was an entirely different matter. All in all, it looked less than reliable but better than nothing. Probably. Bawdy figured the odds of it actually being watertight were about the same odds Bartleby had of walking to Maine.

"Cooking something good for dinner?"

Bartleby looked around, shook his head, "No fire tonight, I guess."

"You don't have a stove?"

"Uh-uh."

"Can borrow mine. Got plenty of fuel."

A shrug, "Still gonna taste like canned chili."

❧

The rain kept on through the night. The temperature didn't drop appreciably and there wasn't much wind, but still at the best of times, there is nothing much enjoyable about sleeping out in the rain. And for Bartleby, this wasn't close to the best of times.

Apparently, the tent came complete with a particularly unpleasant mildewy, mothball stink. Which was nothing a little fresh air couldn't fix. Hopefully.

And he wasn't much surprised to find that the tent leaked,

though he was surprised at how much it leaked. Seemed like some of the water was maybe bubbling up from below, seeping in through the laminated bathtub floor. But mostly it came in from above—all along the low, sagging ceiling and steeply slanted walls. Drops dribbled and dribbles trickled and trickles, well, they pooled along the floor's lowest points. Luckily, he'd set up on a slope, so the water all went towards the back of the tent.

Which begged an interesting question: how could a leaking tent let so much water in and yet, still somehow retain all of that same water. By definition, a leaky tent *leaks*. An unfortunate and undesirable state of being for any tent, but there it is. By logical extension, that simple function of leaking should be a leaky tent's best feature. That is, water should both enter and exit with equal ease. Instead of a catchall, a cistern, a gathering place for water, a leaky tent should be a sieve or conduit, a simple way station, a speedway whooshing water along on its travels.

In the green darkness of the tent, Bartleby balled up tight, endeavoring to keep his feet and sleeping bag up and out of the worst of the wet. Kept shifting his head, trying to avoid the steadiest drips. When one of them got a bead on you it was like Chinese water torture. But even if he could avoid them in flight, there was no avoiding the splash factor. Any sort of lengthy, rejuvenating sleep eluded him. He managed to nap some, mostly in the moments between incoming drops, and that only because he'd become so adept at tuning out when the situation allowed for it. Pretty much perfected that skill at home over the last few years.

In the morning he woke (or at least opened his eyes and

made it official), wrinkled and water-logged. Lay there listening to water plops fall from surrounding tree branches, blipping down into puddles, splattering into the damp carpet of the previous year's foliage. Finally heard Bawdy packing gear away and start in on a Pop-Tart breakfast.

"You awake in there, Bartleby?"

No answer.

"Foggy as anything out here but it stopped raining. Sort of. Can't really tell, actually. So you getting up or what? Only another eight, nine miles to Neels Gap. We push it a little we can be there for a late lunch."

Bartleby unzipped the door of his tent, stuck his head out. Looked like a nappy-headed, sleepy-eyed, all-wet-behind-the-ears groundhog popping up out of its hole. "Think they got pizza?"

"The guide book says it's a hiker oasis. Got a gear shop and hot showers even."

Bartleby wriggled into jeans and a damp sweatshirt, squished sore feet into wet sneakers. Took his gear out of the tent, willy-nillied everything into his pack.

"Sleep good? How'd this circus tent handle the rain last night?"

In answer, Bartleby lifted the empty tent up onto its end. A couple three gallons went pouring out the front door.

"Yowzers, dude. We gotta get you fixed up with some decent gear, you know? Not careful, you're gonna drown out here."

Bartleby folded the tent like a big sloppy burrito, strapped the whole of it to the outside of his pack. Stuffed some last bits of wet gear and clothing inside, forced the top lid closed and precariously perched the Herman Survivors atop everything else. Lashed them into place with their own laces. Let slip a grunt as he hefted the pack up onto his back—like everything else, it was waterlogged and discouragingly heavier than it had been the day before.

"Don't forget about breakfast, the most important meal of the day—specially out here, right? That much less you gotta carry."

Bartleby had forgotten. He turned his back to Bawdy, "Should be something in the left pocket. Can you grab it? If this pack comes off now, I don't think I'm getting it on again."

After a fair bit of fumbling and cursing, Bawdy slapped a tin of sardines into Bartleby's open hand.

"Didn't see nothing else in there, dude."

With no indication that sardines weren't a normal part of his morning routine, Bartleby keyed back the tin's top and poured its contents into his mouth; oily juice, bony finger-sized fillets and whatever else was swimming around in there.

A happier man would've laughed at the look of disgust that swept over Bawdy's face.

✤

"So you never said. What happened to that Bartleby dude? The one in that short story."

"Yeah," Bawdy shook his head, "sorry man, but things... really didn't turn out so well for that Bartleby."

* * *

Blood Mountain was the first real *up* for northbounders coming from Springer. The trail maintainers did what they could to take the bite out: lazy switchbacks zigzagged up the southern approach. Thick stone steps had even been wrestled into place at the turning points where zigs became zags.

Still and all, it was a big-ass climb. There was no getting around that.

Flutterby made the summit without having to rest. The peak was shrouded over in fog; she couldn't see more than a few yards past the point of her nose. Unlike the other shelters she'd seen so far, Blood Mountain Shelter was four-sided and made from stone. Must've been built by the CCC or somebody else with lots of time and plenty of helping hands. It had a couple of window holes and a yawning entrance that looked to have once held a door. Two rooms inside were separated by a stone fireplace and chimney. Standing there in the first room, she wrinkled her nose. At one time it must've been a cozy hut, but that time was back two or three decades ago. Now the shelter was bombed out, graffitied over, rotting away. Dirty, dark and dank. Stunk pretty bad, too. Made Flutterby happy she'd overnighted at Woods Hole Shelter instead.

No place very inviting to sit, so she took a standing break (leaning against the doorframe, mostly out of the rain, but still able to breath fresh air) to eat a snack and peruse the shelter's register.

*

4/11 A black bear barged into the shelter last night and
        dragged off six freakin food bags. Lucky for him we
        were close to a resupply or I mighta had to go Stone
        Cold Steve Austin on his furry ass.

                                                    Peg Master

                              🍁

Flutterby was still a couple hundred yards out when she heard
the first distinct rumblings of vehicles speeding along US-19. She
came out of the woods and took her first look at Neels Gap.

Might've been a cluster of little matching buildings or simply one sprawling complex, she couldn't tell at a glance. Either
way, it consisted of boxy gray stone walls trimmed out in a
nice deep green. Looked like the AT actually disappeared into
a tunnel that went under the building. The whole thing
would've been an impressive sight, stately even, if it weren't for
the ragtag hiker rabble milling around out front.

All told there were three or four dozen. A more motley
gathering of misfits and missionaries, old timers, new-agers,
long-haired loners, runaways, ragamuffins and reprobates,
duds, dropouts, wandering gypsy-freaks and straight up hiker
trash was not to be found this side of Trail Days.

Mostly, these thru-hiker hopefuls were chanting, "Bar-
tle-by! Bar-tle-by!"

That funny little guy with the bad, feathered mullet—Bawdy
he was calling himself now—seemed to be leading the chant

while passing a pair of big yellow boots over to the guy she'd met on the stairs back at Amicalola. The man who'd inadvertently given Flutterby her trail name. That must be Bartleby. They stood beneath a great tree whose bud-less branches were adorned with dozens of old pairs of shoes left dangling from high limbs. A shoe tree.

Bartleby hucked the yellow boots up at the tree, but the toss was well short of even the lowest branch. The crowd ate this up, started getting into the chant. Bawdy retrieved the boots and Bartleby lofted them again. Underhanded and up high, right into the thick of things. Initially, the boots caught, looked to be safely snagged, but momentum carried the second boot swinging over the bough and down they came, tumbling and clodding together.

"Bar-tle-by! Bar-tle-by!"

The third throw, a charmed overhand, sent the boots cartwheeling in a lofty arc. They bounced off one branch, slipped another and another, until finally catching for good. This earned a roar from the crowd.

Flutterby found this absurd scene strangely moving. The few times she'd crossed the poor guy's path, he was shambling around like the living dead. Even during the boot-toss, Bartleby's eyes looked dull and glazed. A bit like how patients went under anesthesia and sometimes their minds shut down before their bodies. She'd seen this happen where patients keep looking around and talking for five or ten minutes, but they couldn't see your hand in front of their face or answer even a simple question. Like maybe somehow the wires connecting brain and soul had been snipped.

* * *

The bunkroom was down in a dingy basement. Twenty dollars got you a brief shower in a damp bathroom with a door that wouldn't quite latch, sleeping space on an old, stained single mattress and the privilege of sleeping in snoring distance of nineteen other hikers. By the time Bawdy arrived, only top bunks were still available. He didn't complain.

After scrubbing himself thoroughly in the shower, he realized he didn't have anything close to a decent outfit without putting his dirty hiking clothes back on. Had to make do with his sky blue thermal tights under green palm tree print boxer shorts (so as to hide away any sausage-smuggling), a maroon fleece vest, bright yellow Crocs (50% off) and, because it was still misty and raw out, his striped wool hat of many colors.

Cut quite the absurd figure, yet nobody batted an eye. He fit right in.

His bunkmate went by Coyote. A sharp-tongued, fast talker with brusque East Coast sensibilities and a certain insatiable glint in his eyes. Bawdy found him appealingly repulsive. Coyote was snipping the tags off his clothes and gear. Claimed it would save him at least half an ounce in pack weight.

Blitz lay holding his stomach in the bunk under Bartleby. He was half out of it and letting off sickly little groans of pleasure. The German farm boy reached Neels Gap in time to take advantage of his first official trail magic. He didn't seem to have a good handle on the underlying concept of trail magic or the phrase itself, but one word Blitz did understand was "free." As in, this do-gooder church group was putting on a free lunch feed for hikers; grilling up and handing out a couple hundred juicy-thick burgers with plenty of fixings. With his first burger in hand (and a bite or two already in mouth), Blitz circled around to the back of the line for another. All told, he'd scored and scarfed nine decked out cheeseburgers. Now it was all he could do to lay on his bunk, contentedly moaning and mumbling about having eaten "Most."

When Bawdy went sniffing around for his share of the free lunch, he found the do-gooders were fresh out of food and packing up.

Aggravated that he'd missed the burger feed, Bawdy continued on to the store. It was bustling with activity. Various books and stationary, woodsy crafts and touristy cotton clothes were arranged for sale in the front room. The gear shop was located in the back. That's where all the action was. Had maybe a dozen backpackers in varying states of despair and disrepair. Now with a few day's experience under their belts, hikers were frantic to upgrade, swap or otherwise reconfigure their packs. Removing or replacing old, heavy, inappropriate or entirely unnecessary stuff with new stuff, lighter stuff, more effective, better fitting stuff.

Seventeen ounce hand-pump water filtration systems were traded out for three ounce Aquamira purification drops. Out went the leathery wine-botas, the travel coffee mugs, the nested aluminum multi-pot cooking sets. In came plastic water bladders and titanium cook pots. The recently purchased steel-shanked, vibram-soled hiking boots were just too heavy and hard on the feet. So they were mailed home and replaced by lightweight hiking shoes and heavy-duty sneakers. Cottony sweatshirts, fleecy jackets and various woolen layers were swapped out for silky thermals and downy pullovers.

One woman, going by the name Squib-Squab, had tears running down her cheeks and the disgorged contents of her backpack spread across the floor. One of the shop's gear experts sat with her, patiently advising which gear she "really" needed. The metal framed 5x7 of her husband and kids did not fall into that category. Neither did the binoculars, the full-sized King James, the family-sized tube of Crest, the portable hand-crank radio or the five pound zero-degree sleeping bag.

This paring down, this letting go of possessions, of home and of previous selves was a painful process for her, for everyone, but it was hopeful too. Adjusting and adapting was about positive action; rising anew from the ashes, invigorated and with dramatically lighter loads. Ultimately, by streamlining and shucking dead weight, hikers exponentially improved their chances of reaching the promised land—Mt. Katadhin.

When Bawdy found his way to the food aisle, he really could've kicked himself for missing the free burgers. After three days and nights of eating lousy camp food, he'd been looking forward to a gorge. Turned out, the dining options before him couldn't quite accommodate that. It was all camping food. Granola bars, candy bars and energy bars. Jerky, Chex-mix, mac and cheese, Knorr dinners and ramen soups. Microwave pizza was the closest thing he found to a greasy hot meal.

Not wanting to make any hasty culinary decisions, he went to the counter to get change for the laundry machines.

"Yeah, let me get four quarters."

"You doing laundry? It's three bucks," the kid at the register said.

Together, the two machines only cost a dollar. Bawdy had already checked.

"I am doing laundry, but I only need four quarters."

The kid plopped a plastic baggy of white powder down on the counter. "The extra dollar is for soap."

There had been plenty of unused soap bags lying around the laundry room. "Thanks, but I don't need soap."

"Gotta buy the soap. Package deal. Laundry costs three bucks."

"The machines only take four quarters."

"The soap costs a dollar and the four quarters for the machines make it a grand total of three dollars," kid was unabashed, almost smug about this.

For the last many years of his life, Bawdy had been thoroughly tangled in the sticky webs, mired deep in the mud that was literary academia. Each semester, he'd taught two low-level English courses while simultaneously advancing his own studies. Most recently, he'd navigated the ungodly morass that is a thesis committee to earn his doctorate. For each of those semesters he'd debated points of literary inanity with colleagues, rebuffed the complaints of disgruntled students and effectively negotiated with the gaggle of prickly, preening contrarians that were his academic mentors. He'd been able to do all of this successfully because he was quick-witted, lightning-tongued and came equipped with an easily accessible sense of self-righteous indignation. He was a man who was happiest when speaking his mind with a voice that cracked like the Pharaoh's own whip when he wanted it to.

Sometimes though, even these prodigious gifts hadn't been enough to get him through. In the darkest hours, he fell back on *the* prime tenet of survival in the University circuit. To win an argument, one simply need talk louder and longer than everyone else.

"Hold up," Bawdy started. "Are you saying I've gotta pay two dollars for soap I don't want or I can't get change for the laundry?"

"Soap only costs a dollar."

"So, if it costs a buck for quarters and a buck for soap, then what's the third buck for?"

"Doing laundry." By this time, a certain glaze of resigned boredom had slipped into the kid's eyes. Bawdy had seen this look a couple million times from his students. It pushed him over the edge.

"This soap I don't want obviously comes from some super-econo-family-sized barrel that costs about fourteen bucks. Which you now are divvying up and hawking off for a profit margin so unholy, it'd make crack dealers crap themselves with jealousy. Which is bad, but not as bad as the phantom third dollar you're trying to squeeze out of me. Kinda runs contrary to this whole hiking thing, doesn't it? Simplify, get back to nature, less is more."

Bawdy stopped for a breath and glared at the cashier, "You know what else? It really chaps my fat ass."

His outburst concluded, Bawdy brandished his dollar bill as aggressively as ever a tubby, mullet-headed Midwestern scholar was able. He stormed out the door muttering phrases like "company store exploitation" and "bald-faced shysters."

✳

"Greedy bastards charged me a buck for holding my mail-drop," Coyote said, simultaneously commiserating and fanning Bawdy's fire. He had such a wide, toothy grin it was easy to see where his name came from. "And this bunkroom smells like old man piss. You know half of us are gonna have bed bugs tomorrow."

"It's disgusting," Bawdy agreed.

Blodgett, an older, frosty-haired hiker, held up a new backpack, "Found this online for almost half the price, but," he shrugged, "I needed it now, not in three to five business days."

"Everything's marked up crazy cuz there ain't nowhere else for us to go."

"Got us in a choke-hold here," Bawdy growled.

"Right by the *balls*," Coyote agreed with emphatic relish.

"I feel like I should do something."

"We could pour concrete into the washer or," Coyote grinned, "or toss a brick through that big front window tonight."

"I was thinking of writing a letter—I write a mean letter."

"You know," Coyote rapped his fist against the cold stone wall, his eyes narrowed to sly little slits, "with enough gasoline, I bet we could burn this place to the ground."

The thought that this Coyote character might be a bit offbalance flittered through Bawdy's mind for the first of what would prove to be many, many times.

Flutterby padded over from her bunk in a far corner. She handed Bawdy a quarter, "Or you could just go around, borrow three more quarters and quietly do laundry without paying The Man his money."

❉ ❉ ❉

Bartleby's feet were clean and dry, disinfected as best as he could manage and elevated above his head at the far end of his bunk. Might not be looking any better yet, but it wasn't like he had a real destination or any kind of hurry to get there. One of the hostel's cats had wormed itself into his armpit. It purred like a chainsaw.

He'd spent the evening dozing on his bunk until Finger Pickin' Good started up stepping an Irish harp through its paces. It was rumored she hoped to pay her way northward by playing crowds and passing the hat. The harp plugged into a portable amp, a little black box she sat on while plucking. Harp and amp together weren't *too* big, maybe a couple feet tall, maybe twelve pounds, but still, it didn't look fun to carry. At best, it was an awkward load. Especially since Finger Pickin' Good was just a smidge over five feet and barely a hundred and five pounds after shoveling down Thanksgiving dinner.

Shortly after the music stopped, Bartleby became aware of a clutch of people whispering together by the bunkroom doorway. Bawdy and Coyote and a short guy he'd never seen before. Fearing it had something to do with him, Bartleby rolled over, faced the wall and hoped they'd go away.

No luck.

There was a tap on his shoulder. It was Bawdy, looking pensive.

"Hey, dude. Listen. Not trying to be too forward here, cross any lines, but see the little guy with the ponytail? He's thru-hiked a coupla times already. He knows what he's doing out here. I asked him to come over, give you a shake down. Go through your gear, see where you might be able to save some weight. Figure you won't do it yourself, and, well, it can't hurt, right?"

The little guy stepped close. He was Napoleon short, with a big strong jaw. Had his glossy black hair tied back into a well-brushed ponytail.

"I'm the Original Grand Poohbah. You can call me Poohbah or OGP, but *do not* call me lil' Poo. Thru-hiked in '97, '01, and again in '04. Within six minutes of my arriving here, the owner came out and asked me if I wanted to work the shop, help out for a few days. Which should tell you that I know my shit."

Bartleby leaned up on an elbow, followed along as best as he could.

"Right off, you're gonna need a new backpack. First, this thing's a Dana Design Terraplane. Probably close to twenty-years old, should be in a museum somewhere. It is old school and bomb-proof but was designed to carry the kitchen sink. This thing weighs maybe eight pounds empty. My pack weighs less than two. And what's worse, your Terraplane's got more than twice the capacity. Which you might think is good, but it's not—the less capacity, the less you can carry. And aside from actually reaching Maine, carrying less is about the most important goal out here.

"Second, I saw you come lurching in. Your pack doesn't fit for shit. Not by a long shot. Got some cramping, fatigue in your back and neck? Shoulders seem like they're gonna be sheared off by the straps, right? Hipbelts are meant to rest on the hip bone, transfer weight down to your hips, instead of making the back and shoulders do the carrying. *Yours* is riding up around your ribs, which means there's no load transfer happening. Do yourself a favor and get a new pack in the morning. Pretty much anything is going to be a major improvement. And after that, well—let's see what all you got in here."

Without waiting for permission, Poohbah upended Bartleby's pack, splashed its innards on the floor. Sorted things here and there, tossed stuff straight into the garbage (food wrappers and empty cans). When he was done, the remaining gear and clothes were separated into two piles. The big pile consisted of Bartleby's tent, the raincoat, most of his clothes and various equipment, implements and mementos. Into the little pile went his sleeping bag, flashlight and a few other bits of "gear" that Angie had sent along.

Poohbah tossed his ponytail and smiled greasily. Confidence rose off of him like the warm stink from an old boot. "Let me start off by saying that I've hiked over seven thousand miles and this is, without any doubt or exaggeration, the absolute worst pile of crap gear I've ever come across. It's so bad in fact, I'm going to step out on a limb and talk to you as if you don't know anything about anything. Okay?"

He rapped knuckles against a metal canteen, "You'll want to have the capacity to carry two or three liters of water, but you don't need those expensive hose and bladder setups. Coupla one-liter plastic bottles'll be fine. Probably want a cook stove. Alcohol stoves are simple and cheap. Food wise, you should stick to pasta, noodles and plenty of snack bars. Nuts are a nice diversion. And if for some insano reason you're serious about carrying canned food," Poohbah held the KitchenAid can-opener that had come straight from Bartleby's utensil drawer at home, between two fingers like it was a stinking carcass, "at least get yourself a p-38. You know p-38s? Those little army

50

can openers that weigh less than a nickel. You can wear one around your neck on a string.

"You're gonna need a shirt and shorts that aren't cotton. Coupla pair of wool socks. Water purification. Drops, a pump, whatever. Warm clothes: some kinda windproof jacket—either insulated or waterproof, your pick. And a set of thermals. I like thumbholes, you like thumbholes? Yeah, so maybe get yourself something with thumbholes."

"Now this little pile," Poohbah continued, "is all the stuff I think you should seriously consider replacing or getting rid of entirely. I mean," he held up a matching knife, fork and spoon, "this is real flatware. Melt it down, mail it home, get rid of it. Get yourself a Lexan spoon for two bucks. Shave a pound off right there. Don't know what kind of budget you're working with, but a titanium pot is a good idea. And at twenty dollars, a simple LED headlamp is really worth the upgrade too. Toss these D cells. Like it or not, that's my professional opinion."

Bartleby nodded, "Can you adjust this pack?"

"If anyone can make this junker fit you, it's me. Seriously though, you don't want it. It's bigger and heavier and older than half the mountains we're gonna walk over. I mean, for Christ's sake, it's a *Terraplane*."

Bartleby shrugged.

"Okay, fine. We'll see what's what after dinner. Alright?"

Bartleby nodded. Poohbah flashed a condescending my-work-is-done-here smile and started away.

"That's really not so bad, right, B?" Bawdy said. "You get to keep the whole big pile."

"Actually," Poohbah called back, "everything in the big pile should go straight into the nearest fire. Don't think about it, don't mail it home, don't put it into the hiker box. Be like poisoning the well. Some other fuzzy-nutted newbie might come along and pick it up. I mean—a cotton beach towel? And that tent alone has to weigh nine pounds." A derisive snort. "Absolute crap."

It must've been like three in the morning, but Flutterby didn't bother to check. Just lay there, stock still, so as to keep the plastic crinkling of the mattress to a bare minimum. The middle of the night wasn't anything new for her, but passing it in a dreary basement filled with strangers was. If she'd been home, she would've gotten up, taken a bath or Googled names from her high school yearbook. Or she might've gone for an early morning run, burned through a thousand crunches, and set her mind to denying that somehow she'd married a man who didn't want to touch her.

Bawdy left Neels Gap early. First-one-out-of-bed early. Before-the-sun-was-up early. Everything looked gritty and gray in the pre-dawn light. Must've rained in the night. The air was chill and wet; the trail was splotched with puddles.

He wondered briefly if he'd ever see Bartleby again. Which led to wondering if he'd been too presumptuous in subjecting Bartleby to Poohbah's overly-haughty but otherwise spot-on, steel-brushed scrutiny. The OGP. Little guy was a complete and utter wank, but he did know his gear. And Bartleby had certainly needed some advice and stiff shove in the right direction. Poor guy might be the only person in the entire history of the AT who'd been forcibly made to hike alone and against his will.

As the AT rose up and sawtoothed its way along ridges, Bawdy's legs warmed to the work and his brain slowly emptied of thoughts. Birds sang and the sun slowly crested the eastern horizon.

When he saw Flutterby set off hiking, Coyote quick packed up and followed right after. Figured to catch up with her in a mile or two. Sniff around a bit, see what was what. Great looking girl. He'd already tried to start up a conversation, and she'd been maybe a little cool. But that was fine, he wasn't easily deterred.

He was a wiry 5'8". Had already come to consider himself a fast hiker, and he wasn't wrong. Stride wasn't anything special, but he was a real quick stepper. No surprise there. Eating, talking, and now walking—pretty much did everything fast.

Would catch her in a mile or two. Easy bet.

When at last Bartleby woke, the hostel was largely empty. Most everyone was already up and gone. Of the few stragglers, he was the only one still in bed. Or still in his damp sleeping bag on a stained, moldy smelling mattress as the case may be. He'd slept right on through the noise and light and general commotions of some twenty-odd hikers stuffing away taffeta sleeping bags, zipping zippers and packing up all their worldly possessions. A minor miracle of sorts.

Using the opener Poohbah had put into the "out" pile, Bartleby opened a can of Spaghetti-O's. Took his sweet time swallowing little meatballs whole and slurping down that oddly tangy sauce. When he was done, he took out the bank envelope Angie had given him. It was still sealed. Tore the top off, counted the bills inside. They added up to eight hundred sixty dollars. Not nearly what she should have gotten for the guitar, but really, deep down, he couldn't much care. He hadn't played the thing in five years, hadn't looked at it since before his father died.

He picked up the can opener, studied it a moment and clunked it into the garbage.

❦ ❦ ❦

"You get water back at that Pigpen Gap?"

"Zowie. You scared the hell outta me, Coyote. Can't go sneaking like that. As if my heart isn't under enough strain here."

"Yeah, okay."

"Hogpen."

"Huh?"

"We just hiked up from Hogpen Gap."

"Whatever. How far off trail was the water?"

"Hundred feet maybe. Good flow too."

"Shit. Shoulda stopped, I guess. Almost out. Was trying to catch that Flutterby chick, but I musta flew by her somehow."

"Doubt it. She passed me like an hour ago."

"Seriously? I been humping along here pretty good."

"Maybe you can catch her at the next shelter. We got to be coming up on Low Gap in a mile or two."

In the lower and middle elevations, pastel green leaf buds were beginning to appear on the tips of tree branches. The recent rainy weather was encouraging the spring cycle of growth.

"Name's Bawdy, right?

"Uh-huh."

"Why'zat? You swear a lot?"

"Guess so. Sorta. Didn't really think so, but—"

"I fucking swear a lot too, dude."

"That's...cool."

"Just saying. Not like you got the market cornered on cursing."

❀ ❀ ❀

Bartleby walked out of the Neels Gap tunnel and into a sunbright noon. He wore khaki hiking shorts, a wicking t-shirt and wool socks with his old sneakers. Still looked sludgy-headed and empty-eyed, but now at least he looked like a sludgy-headed and empty-eyed hiker, instead of some homeless fellow with dirty, droopy jeans.

Pretty much everything about his pack looked better too. The shoulder straps were functionally loose, helping to keep the pack upright but otherwise letting the weight settle naturally where it should. And the waist belt rode his hips roughly where it was supposed to. The Terraplane no longer leaned precariously, no longer towered overhead, no longer bulged like a bullfrog's throat. All malevolent spirits appeared to have been exorcised and tamed, befriended or bribed off.

It wasn't a perfect rig, was never going to win, place or even show in any best pack contest with more than three contestants. Still too heavy. Still too big and bulky. But at least Bartleby no longer looked like a clown, didn't look anymore out of place than so many of the other hiker-hopefuls who knew nothing about the woods or camping but were still attempting to make one great big go of this pilgrimage to Maine.

He dumped his jeans and his flannel shirt into a garbage can. Then, before he was tempted to rescue his favorite shirt, he set off northward with only the clack-clicking of STD's hiking poles for company.

Low Gap Shelter was situated amidst a marshy spread of low, washed out land. It had, for some unfathomable reason, been painted a demonic, schoolhouse red. Purple-green heads of skunk cabbage surrounded the shelter. They helped explain the sour, stale, skunky stink filling the air. There was a picnic table out front. A crinkled codger of an old man was sitting, picking the shell from a hard-boiled egg when Flutterby arrived.

Weather and water and whatever else over the years had been particularly unkind to the table. The thing drooped and swayed like an old rope bridge.

Without thinking too much about it, Flutterby whunked her pack down onto the seat plank. She was just making to sit next to the old guy as the table see-sawed up in front of her. It might've actually flipped over if she'd gotten her weight fully down on the bench.

"Whoa!" the old guy hollered. A crescent of eggshells arced through the air. He went over backwards, flat on his back with his knobby knees pointed skyward. The table settled with a heavy *ker-crunk* and the ominous wobble of rotting wood.

"Oh my god," Flutterby bent down and leaned over him, concern wrinkling her face. She made to help him up.

"Not so fast," he wheezed. Made a strained, squinty-eyed face, like a badly-bearded Popeye getting his prostate checked. Put his hands out, patted the ground to get his bearings. Patted himself, ostensibly checking for busted bones. She kept leaning there, patient and worried that she'd somehow gone and broken this old guy.

"Let me just see if," he rasped, "everything feels like it should."

When she felt his hands pat familiarly on her ass, she figured out he probably wasn't hurt all too badly.

"Yep," he gap-tooth grinned, "guess everything feels pretty darned good."

Flutterby quickly extricated herself, but couldn't help smiling. As a nurse, she crossed paths with plenty of overly-familiar old men. Used to be they skeeved her out. These last few years, she'd found their harmless advances to be strangely comforting.

"Been so long since a pretty young thing's come along and knocked me off my feet," he went on, "but see here, it's like I'm always saying, the trail provides just what ya need most."

When he was quite ready, he got to his feet with little

difficulty. Retrieved his egg from where it had rolled in the dirt. Brushed it off and took a bite. He was lankily tall, with an animated face under a gleaming bald dome. His thin beard didn't quite cover over a nickel-sized liverspot on his jaw.

"Well," he grinned, "that was invigorating."

Might've been Flutterby's imagination, but the crotch of his pants seemed suspiciously bulged.

"Glad to see everything's still in working order," she coughed. "I'm Flutterby, by the way."

"It's been quite nice to meet you, Miss Flutterby," he said. Then he winked, "You can call me Trouble. Old Man Trouble."

When Coyote and Bawdy rolled into Low Gap Shelter they were spitting f-bomb euphemisms back and forth as fast as they could think of them.

"Flipping."

"Flapping."

"Frig."

"Focker."

"Fudge."

"Firetruck."

"Motherfather."

"Shut the front door," Coyote hollered. Then, less loudly and to Flutterby, "Where you running off to?"

Flutterby was just shouldering her pack. "Blue Mountain. Old Man Trouble sweet talked me into going further. Says it's easy hiking. Either of you two pussyfoots coming with?"

Coyote quick dipped his water bottles into the stream and scampered off close on Flutterby's heels.

Left alone, Bawdy dropped his pack. Scanned the shelter area, found it wanting and lonely. Shook his head, sighed slowly and pulled his pack back on.

✤

Whoever he was, Old Man Trouble wasn't a liar. The hiking *was* easy. The trail largely followed an old forest road, a wide pathway with mostly even footing. It had a steady, but somehow pleasant incline with a sharp drop-off immediately to the east.

Still, though, Blue Mountain Shelter was 7.2 miles beyond Low Gap, for a grand total of eighteen miles from Neels Gap. A feat that had never been on Bawdy's radar. Certainly wasn't something he was physically prepared for at this point in his hike. Crusty white rings of salt appeared around his armpits and his waist. Sweat dripped off his brow, his nose, the stubbly hairs on his chinny, chin, chin. His legs felt dumbly numb and entirely out of his control. They kept shuffling one foot in front of the other, seemingly without his say so. He wondered about that for almost a mile, but didn't dare try and assert control over them. Feared he wouldn't be able to get them started up again if he did actually rein them in.

He wasn't mentally prepared for hiking eighteen miles either. Tried but never managed to catch up with Coyote. Which, while disappointing, came as no surprise considering how fast Coyote had scurried off after Flutterby. Bawdy didn't pass anyone going north or south or even cutting across on side trails. No turkey hunters, no trail angels, no trooping scouts.

Not one single soul. Nobody. No body. And it might've been his mind playing tricks, but the woods seemed too quiet, almost eerily so. There were no bird calls, no madly dashing chipmunks, no tree branches creaking in the wind. He was stranded and alone, with only his over-active imagination for company.

When he did stop to take a break, he was so spooked by what he'd come to understand was a preternatural stillness, he couldn't help but start up hiking again right away. Hot footing it too. With at least three miles still to go, Bawdy'd convinced himself that something horrible (i.e. apocalyptic) had happened and somehow he was the last being left alive on the planet. With two miles to go, he was looking back over his shoulder a couple of times every minute utterly convinced that whatever foulness had come for everyone else, would be creeping up on him any moment. With less than one mile between Bawdy and the shelter on Blue Mountain, fat tears of fear and manic fatigue glistened in his eyes. Despite passing white blazes with clockwork regularity, he convinced himself that he'd gone off trail, gotten turned around and thoroughly lost in the wild wilderness of northern Georgia.

He stumbled around a bend in the trail, mumbling unintelligibly. Was so worked up it took him a moment to process and recognize the shelter's silhouette for what it was.

Made his lurching way down the side trail to the shelter, wide-eyed and not entirely convinced he wasn't experiencing a mirage, delusion or some rotten figment of his demented imagination. Flutterby was closest, so all but sobbing now, he went and hugged her fiercely.

"Hey now—wait a minute," Coyote called over.

Register: Blue Mountain Shelter

4/9   Hiked eighteen ENDLESS miles yesterday.
      Unplanned, unnecessary and definitely unhealthy.
      Some parts went numb (thank god) but everything
      else hurts. Am so stiff this morning, I fell over
      coming out of my tarp. Literally...fell...right...over.
      Old Man Trouble keeps going on how "the trail
      provides." I'd like to see it provide me with some
      serious opiates in the VERY near future.
                                          —Bawdy

When Bartleby finally got there, it was early evening and Low Gap Shelter was crowded. Close to twenty people buzzing around. He was lucky to find an open spot on the shelter floor.

Bartleby emptied his pack and set to monkeying with his new alcohol stove. After successfully lighting it and setting water to boil, he sat and killed time watching his fellow hikers.

Crazy Ray and a handful of others were standing a little ways off, kicking a red, yellow and green knit hacky-sack and passing a fatty around and around and around. One older guy was marching here and there, collecting dead wood for a fire. He had a serious looking hatchet belted at his waist. Yessiree Bob was winded and seeing stars from blowing his sleeping pad up. The Wabash Cannonball was off by himself, leaned up against a tree trunk, talking tearfully into his phone. At the picnic table, Chunky Dunk, a dangerously obese woman was stitching a split seam back together. Next to her, Again was telling the story about why he'd gone off trail back in '05. It was a convoluted story, torturously told in a droning, Eeyore voice. Ostensibly, Again's audience was Blodgett, Blitz and the Freakin' Deacon, but only Freakin' was listening to anything Again had to say. Blitz had his earbuds plugged in and turned up. Blodgett was asking Poohbah about the upcoming hostels.

"You know, when I first hiked, hostels were few and far between. Nobody got into it to make money; it was nothing but a labor of love. Back then, the owners really understood this whole escape-back-to-nature thru-hiking thing, and best as they could, they supported It. *It* didn't support them. They'd do anything for you, and if they somehow managed to break even, it was a banner year. Blueberry Patch, Kincora and a couple others up north—they're still fighting that good fight."

He spat into the firepit.

"Nowadays, hostels have sprung up like roadside weeds. Most are out to make a quick buck. Not trying to improve the thru-hiking experience, not trying to help lost souls find themselves or even to reach Maine. They're just trying to suck money out of our wallets as we pass through. They'll do anything for ya—for a few bucks. Doesn't make them bad places, but they sure aren't anything special.

"And it's not just hostels. Lots of trail towns are taking their cue from Damascus, setting up little weekend festivals to be like Trail Days. Making the AT feel like one big amusement park ride. Everyone moves along at the same pace, stays at the same places, has the same exact experiences."

Poohbah interrupted himself to point out a trail etiquette faux pas. "Whose pack is this? Somebody needs to get this thing out of here. How about a little consideration, people? A trail crew didn't go to all the effort of building a picnic table out here in the middle of the woods, just so someone's pack could have a seat."

When nobody claimed the pack, Poohbah jabbed at it with his elbow. Thing toppled in slow motion like a tree. Hit the ground with a sickly *flwomp-bronk* and enough force to maybe break stuff. Probably not, but it didn't sound good.

After assuming the recently vacated seat, Poohbah started running a brush through his hair with a certain feline fastidiousness, "It's called trail etiquette newbs: learn it or leave it."

❦

At some ungodly hour, five or six am, a phone alarm burst into sing-song. A children's choir started singing at top volume. Something about rising and shining and giving god their glory, glory.

"Sorrysorrysorrysorrysorry," the Freakin' Deacon said as he scrambled for the phone buried in his pack. Took him most of eternity to finally find it and turn it off. "Sorry all. I swear I turned this damn thing off yesterday."

"You're going to hell, Deacon," Poohbah grumbled.

❦

Bartleby hadn't gotten very far the next morning when he caught up to Chunky Dunk. Big as she was, there was no slipping around her so he hiked along behind for a while. She never heard him, what with all the ragged wheezing and wet rasps coming out of her.

Wasn't too long before she reached a trailside log. It was only after she had settled herself down, did she realize he'd been drafting along behind.

"Y'all been back there long?"

Bartleby mustered what he figured would pass for a friendly nod and made to hike on. Chunky had sweat streaming down everywhere: her face, her neck, her bare arms. From the knees up, her pants were soaked through.

"So what ya think? Imma die out here?"

Bartleby couldn't help but pull up short.

"See, I tol' myself I'd keep walking 'til I dropped dead or got skinny. Figured I had a one in five chance a gettin' skinny, but hell, now I'm out here an survived my first week, maybe it's more like one in four. This here," she grabbed a hunk of belly fat, "it ain't no way to live. Gettin' so I'd rather be dead than fat."

If there ever was an appropriate response to this opening salvo, Bartleby was not the man to come up with it. He stood there, dumb as a dopey heifer.

"Figure, *if* I don't die," Chunky continued, "Imma be good and skinny by Maine. Change my name to Skinny Dip. Be jumping into every lake and river I can find too. Buck-ass naked and skinny as a schoolgirl. Paints a pretty picture don't it?" She gave Bartleby a challenging look, "Y'all just see if I don't."

Imagining herself as a water nymph frolicking and splashing her way to Katahdin was enough to start Chunky laughing. It started slow and low, somewhere deep inside, but steadily gathered momentum and rose up towards the surface. It was cheery and infectious—Bartleby couldn't help but join in with her.

At best it was gallows humor. Chunky Dunk's predicament wasn't funny in the least. Obviously different than his, but no less tragic.

He certainly hadn't planned on saying anything, hadn't even been thinking about things, but somehow Chunky's candor knocked the lid loose. "So you got a lot on the outside," he said, "I'm all empty inside. Used to feel dried up and dead, but now I don't feel nothing. Wife dumped me off at Amicalola, thinks hiking might somehow help. Don't see how. And you know what else?"

"What?"

"I'm only still hiking because I can't figure anything else to do."

❧

Walter found a bathroom around the side of the Amicalola Visitor Center.

In there, alone and illuminated by a flickering florescent bulb, he pulled a hooded sweatshirt off over his head. Underneath, a plaid flannel shirt and faded blue jeans. Down low he wore work boots with thick yellow outsoles and deep lugs.

Walter stood before the poorly lit mirror. A moment of reflection.

When not slouched down, he was an easy six feet tall. His torso had turned thick and pudgy. This wasn't big bones or muscle mass, it was soft white flesh. It was late-night ice cream, third helpings of Angie's lasagna and french fries for lunch. Since college, weight had been a battle for him, but this last year or so it had become a rout. Beneath fresh stubble, his face was ashen and pore-pocked. His unremarkable hair was shot through with hints of gray but still mostly where it was supposed to be. Murky eyes. His license called them hazel, but that wasn't right. They were darker. The first crinkly hints of crow's feet were coming in at the corners. A sharp little nose looked out of place against the bleary backdrop of his rounded face. He was thirty-eight and at that moment, he looked much older. It wasn't so long ago that people guessed he was six or seven years younger than his age, but not now. Not anymore.

Used to be he was lanky and knobby-jointed. Goofy looking, but in that gentle way that some women settled for. Had a too big smile, that came easy and honest. Way back when, he'd stayed out of trouble and laughed a lot. Spent four years on his high-school track team. Long jump, triple, high. Nothing special, no records or ribbons, but still, he could move, had some spring in those long legs of his.

Slid through four years at the University of Connecticut back before it was a good school. Graduated with a biology degree, moved home, took his only job offer—assistant manager of a pharmacy. Convinced himself it was sort of in his field of interest. Took him a few years to realize it wasn't. Took a few more to admit that aloud, and still a few more to think maybe he wanted to teach high school science. Eventually started taking classes at night. Finished up the coursework just in time to take over the family business.

The family business was residential construction. Walter's father was a general contractor with a good reputation and pride in his work. The housing market was bubbling and he propped up spec homes fast as he

66

could buy land. Poured any profits right back into the business. Had nine properties in some stage of development when his truck went off the road one night. He died after a few days in intensive care.

In general, it was sudden and terrible and all that. For Walter, it was far worse. With so much money tied up and suddenly at risk, it was apparent that someone had to take up the reins. He was close and available and as qualifications went, those were the only ones that mattered. And so instead of teaching science, Walter started building houses. Finished off and moved most of the inventory, had gone ahead and started a few new projects when the housing market collapsed down around him. He choked on what was left.

Staring there at himself in the drafty bathroom, Walter ached with the long unraveling. He was alone now, and lost. This was one of those rare moments where he figured it would be acceptable, even appropriate for a man to cry. Had always regretted making it through his father's funeral with dry eyes. Felt like maybe if he'd cried back then, somehow things might've turned out differently. Figured crying now couldn't hurt. Stood there, willing and waiting but nothing came. Like an abandoned burrow, Walter was all dark and dry inside.

A ranger came in to use the bathroom, snapping Walter out of his trance at the mirror.

"Hiking? Heading out?"

Walter grunted.

"Going all the way? You know, been staffed here almost ten years and I still get this little pang of jealously," the ranger called from inside a stall, "every time one of you thru-hikers sets off up the falls. Footloose and free as birds. Rambling along, easy as you like, communing with nature, becoming one with the woods and all. Six months of fresh air and—"

Walter grabbed his sweatshirt and retreated outside.

There was an archway around back made from rough stone and lots of mortar. According to the sign, the arch represented the beginning of the Approach Trail. From here it was almost nine miles up to the top of Springer Mountain. He stood there a moment, assessing options.

Which, far as he could see, weren't really all that numerous or promising. Of course, there was the easy out: toss himself under a bus. This wasn't too appealing even when he'd had a halfway decent life insurance policy. Also, it seemed to require levels of initiative and motivation he hadn't possessed in forever. A second option was to limp home again by whatever means presented themselves. Plane, train, taxi. This was tempting, except he couldn't expect any kind of welcome. Even if Angie let him in the front door, nothing would've changed. He still would've single-handedly lost everything his father had built. He'd still see that little glint of disappointment in his mother's eyes. Every little thing that had kept him pressed down deep into the recliner for days at a time would still be there, looming overhead.

The only other option was to slink down to his brothers' place in Tampa. They hadn't been close since Mark's wedding. Hadn't talked since the funeral.

And that was it. The entire list; all the options Walter could figure.

He sighed then, a long and defeated huff of hopelessness.

And started walking.

Blodgett was going just fast enough that Bawdy couldn't lose him. He could spurt away and ahead for a bit, but not at any sustainable speed. Eventually, he'd have to slow down or take a break and Blodgett would be there at his elbow again.

There was really nothing for it but to talk to the old guy.

"—and then I figured, if nobody wants me to work for them, I guess it's about time I go out and take a walk in the woods."

"Huh," Bawdy said. And then after a bit, "How'd you get the name Blodgett?"

"Yeah, well, named myself. After a character from one a them old Disney movies. *The Incredible Journey*. It's about two dogs and a cat who set off together to find their owners. The older of the two dogs was this white haired bull terrier named Blodgett. He was steady and real slow, but he didn't have any quit in him. Just kept on. That's me. I just keep on going and don't stop for nothing."

Bawdy had an amazing memory, particularly when it came to trivialities and pop culture detritus. He voraciously consumed movies, books, graphic novels, music and podcasts; really anything he could get his hands on. Remembered pretty much every character, every scene, every lyric and every actor who played every role. Mostly he used this prodigious skill of his to win lots of stupid bar bets.

"He was all gruff and tough, right? Real stiff upper lip?"

"That's him."

"Um, yeah. Sorry to break it to you, Blodgett, but that dog's name was Bodger."

Somewhere north of Unicoi Gap, Bartleby came up on two hikers. There was a piped spring sticking out from under an old gravelly road. The thing tinkled out a quart of water with all the oomph of a senior with prostate problems. The hikers were sitting there at the collected pool filtering water.

"Didn't I tell you not to drink so much?" the guy was saying. He had dull blue eyes and a scraggly-ass beard. It was fully in, but not close to full and made him look cult leader creepy. The couple was young, roughly college age, and they both entirely ignored Bartleby's arrival.

"I was thirsty. I drank my water. Now I need more water. What'd I do wrong this time, Brian?"

And there stretched a pause so pregnant it had to have been carrying a whole litter to term. Each time Brian depressed the handle of the water filter it made a rusty little *EEEEEEEE* squeak. As if even the filter itself was put out at all this bother.

"What'd I say about calling me that? We're on the Appalachian Trail and out here I'm Harebrained and you're Two-Speed Tortoise. And all I'm saying is—we'd be making better time if we didn't have to stop for water every other mile."

"Right up until I collapsed from heat stroke or dehydration or something," she fired back. "Then you'd have to carry me out. And we both know that'd put a real crimp on your pace, wouldn't it?"

The way these two were situated around the water they all but blocked off access to the deepest part of the puddle. Bartleby couldn't just squeeze in and fill up; he had to queue up and wait his turn. He would've hiked on, passed by this little scene, but he'd drunk all his water too and was thirsty enough to stick it out. He thought he recognized the girl and so while standing there, occupied himself with trying to place her. Didn't take too long—there really wasn't an over-abundance of women floating around out on trail. She'd been the girl he'd seen climbing out of the bed of the pickup truck way back at the top of Amicalola Falls. From this close distance, he could see that she was as plumply cute as a baby marmot. Wore a red sports bra and tan shorts. Had two short pig-tails of russet colored hair poking out beneath a straw sun hat.

Harebrained finished pumping water, packed the filter away and stalked off up the trail without another word.

Two-Speed Tortoise looked at Bartleby for the first time.

"You know," she said with a resigned sadness that was instantly recognizable to Bartleby, "If I ever did need any kind of medical attention, I doubt he'd actually stick around to help carry me out."

The kid was big and brawny; corn-fed stock raised alongside some irrigation ditch on the dusty outskirts of Podunk, America. Rounded, meaty shoulders kept post-thick arms and wide, callused hands attached to a strapping torso. He looked like he could take care of himself and any three guys stepping up. For all that, there was an amiable contentedness there in the kid's eyes. If happy-go-lucky wasn't exactly the right phrase, it was close. All of this was so instantly and shiningly obvious to Coyote, he couldn't help but to feel a jealous twinge in the dark, boggy bottom of his soul.

The kid's face was covered in downy wisps, the beginnings of what would undoubtedly be a robust blonde beard. Probably somewhere in his mid-twenties. He wore one of those floppy-brimmed booney hats and a matching beige pixilated camou-flage t-shirt. He sprawled there at the picnic table, pushing buttons on one of those oversized, super smart computer watches when Coyote rolled up to the shelter. He must've been lonely, because he started right in talking.

"Hey what's up, man? They call me Peg Master."

Coyote glanced around the empty shelter area, looking to see who or where *they* might be. Wasn't a soul in sight. "Who calls you that?"

"Everybody. It's my trail name."

"Why would they call you that?"

"'Cuz I'm so good at cribbage. Got a board with me. Seriously. Peg circles around you."

"What kind of board?"

Peg Master gave a long squinting look to see if there was a fool in the conversation. Finally, "Cribbage board."

"That...sounds heavy."

Peg Master actually flexed a bicep, "S'not a problem." His pack was a monster. Looked ship-shape, but crammed full.

"What's in there all?"

"Over there," the kid gestured eastward, "they had us carrying ninety pounds of gear—water, ammo, body armor—all kinds of shit," he waved at his pack, "this ain't nuttin'."

Coyote tried hefting the pack. Probably weighed more than twice his. Seventy pounds at least. "Seriously—you got a body in here? Encyclopedia, maybe?"

"Seriously—you wanna play?"

"Play what?"

"Cribbage."

"Nah."

"Why? I'll teach you. It's easy."

"I play some."

"Yeah? I won two tournaments. Company-wide. That's why they call me Peg Master."

"Nobody calls you that."

"*You* got a trail name?"

"Yep."

A long thoughtful silence ensued. It was broken only by the sounds of Coyote chewing. Finally he said, "You know what, Big Boy?"

"What?"

"I'll play ya when I finish eating." Coyote grinned, "But listen, we gotta play for something."

"Seriously? You wanna bet against an international champ who calls himself Peg Master?"

"See? You gave yourself that name."

"Whatever."

"Just a friendly little wager," here the grin grew wider, toothier. "Keep it interesting, right?"

"What'cha thinking—dime a point?"

"Better."

"Quarter?"

"Better."

"Yeah?"

"We'll play for trail names."

"That's broke-dick, dude. Tol' you, I got one."

"And look who doesn't want to play now."

"I wanna play, but I told you I already got a trail name."

"And I'm telling you, you don't got no trail name. What you got is a plea for help. And so I'm gonna help."

"Help how?"

"Easy. See, if—*when* you win, you validate your claim of

being the Cribbage King or whatever you're calling yourself. Right? Earn some easy local trail cred. Top of that, you get to give me a trail name. Whatever you want—so long as it's not Hairy Hatchet Hole or Dr. Douchenstein or anything that won't fly when someone picks me up for a hitch."

"And?"

"And if I get lucky, happen to squeak one out, well, then I'll give you some sort of honest trail name, something catchy, something that really represents."

"Peg Master represents."

"Not if I beat you it don't."

Peg Master squinted hard and mulled it over.

"I'm fucked if you aren't making some sense, dude. It's broke-dick sense, but alright, let's go—one game. Cut for deal. Low card. Here, I got a four."

"Ace."

❦

When Bawdy arrived, he was huffing like an asthmatic. He plopped down at the shelter edge and took his time catching his breath.

"Heya, Bawdy-boy."

"That was a climb, huh?"

"All the way up, it was," Coyote agreed.

Bawdy waved at the cards scattered all about on the ground. Red and white and ringing round the picnic table like some fifty-odd hemorrhoids circling the world's largest, unluckiest anus. "What's all this?" he asked.

"Bawdy, have you met my friend here?"

"No. Hey."

The kid nodded grimly. When he didn't say anything, Coyote gave him a little prompting nudge.

"Well, shit."

"Come on now," Coyote encouraged.

"Bawdy is it? Hey. I'm...I guess...well, my name's... Skunkers."

The last mile down to GA-76 was a straight shot. Bartleby could hear cars and trucks zooming along well before he ever caught a glimpse of them. Leaves were starting to come in on the trees now; one moment he was enveloped by lush greenery and the next he was standing on black asphalt. On the north side of the road, Two-Speed Tortoise was standing with her thumb out. A shady guy leaned against an old IROC-Z Camaro neaby. Bartleby noticed because it kinda took him back to when Camaros were respectable, or maybe they never were respectable and he was simply too young to know any better. Shady Guy wasn't hiking: had on jeans, a not-so-white wife-beater and mirrored sunglasses.

There weren't any cars coming or going. Bartleby crossed over to Tortoise, "Been here long?"

"Feels like forever. You see Harebrained back on trail anywhere?"

"Uh-uh."

Her face scrunched down into a scowl and her eyes brimmed up with moisture, "He was supposed to wait for me here. It's my first time hitching. This morning I told him I didn't want to do it alone. So he just races right into town and leaves me out here with this dirty d-bag. Oh, Christ," she whispered, "here he comes again."

Shady Guy sauntered up to Bartleby, a can of Budweiser in hand, "Got beers over in my cooler. Want one?"

"Uh-uh."

"Need any weed man?"

"Uh-uh."

Shady Guy's face brightened hopefully, "Ya got any weed?"

"Uh-uh."

"Going into Hiawassee? I can take y'all. Ten bucks each."

"Uh-uh."

"Eight bucks?"

"I already told you to beat it," Tortoise growled. She raised her hiking pole menacingly, "You want a Leki in the eye?"

"That's cool," he said before moseying off back to his IROC.

Tortoise turned back to the road, studiously intent on flagging a hitch. Tried to hide it, but her bottom lip was all aquiver.

Which was like a gut-punch for Bartleby. Instantly reminded him of the last time he'd seen his wife's lip similarly quivering.

✤

Walter slumped in the passenger seat watching the passing countryside with vacant eyes. Seemed like Angie had accelerated again; paradoxically increasing her speed even as the roads shrunk from interstate to county highway to twisty back road.

She checked the GPS when a road sign welcomed them to Lumpkin County, "Twelve more miles."

Walter's only reaction was to slump lower in the seat. Like a jack-o-lantern in November, he looked to be wilting under his own weight.

"You understand I love you, right?" she explained for at least the ninth time. "Wouldn't...couldn't bother with any of this if I didn't."

Walter might've responded with a grunt. He certainly thought about grunting.

"I don't know what else to do. It's gotten so that any day I get you up and out of that goddamn chair is a goddamn victory. Can't do it anymore...won't. Remember how tough it was for us to juggle the kids and everything? Now I'm trying to carry all that and your sad self. It's too heavy. I'm sorry, I'm not...strong enough."

A tear drained down into the hollow of Angie's cheek. All the weight she'd lost these last months, he'd found and then some.

Another few miles dribbled past. Angie yawned big and slugged old, cold coffee. She was uncharacteristically talkative; likely overwhelmed by a combination of caffeine, fatigue and guilt. "Remember my cousin Marlene? Her youngest boy Tommy spent some time out here. Marlene said it really helped to turn him around. Gave him a new perspective on life and everything. I think he's actually signed up for some classes now."

Walter remembered Tommy; remembered how he'd avoided juvenile detention by voluntarily enrolling in a hoods-in-the-woods-tough-love-boot-camp-intervention-program. Which the kid had immediately and absolutely hated. Walter remembered that Tommy had, as a passive protest, turned his bowels off. Somehow willed himself to stop going to the bathroom. Lasted the better part of two weeks before being hospitalized with a fecal impaction. Far as Walter knew, Tommy never stepped foot in the woods again.

"So, you know, I mean...maybe you'll be similarly enlightened, right?"

This time Walter made sure to grunt. Riding that momentum for all it was worth he said, "I really don't want to do this."

His voice was the fathomless blue of the deep Atlantic.

"I know, babe," Angie nodded. "And you don't have to. If you want, I'll turn the car around."

He looked at her.

"Just as soon as you name something you actually wanna do. One single thing you'll honestly and happily engage with. You wanna riverdance? I'll learn how to fiddle. Wanna be an ultimate fighter? Rob banks? Run for congress? From the comfort of that ratty recliner, you could do as well as any of the schnooks we got in office now. Or, or how about a spring fling? Couple of hot dates with a pretty little thing in a sundress? I could probably set something up, help you get started. I'm serious, Walter. Anything."

Walter stared out the window. The trees were bare. No buds, no leaves, no signs of life. The sun was just coming up and casting long, grasping shadows over the red-tinged ground.

"After the business died, you stopped looking for work, stopped leaving the house, stopped brushing your teeth. I mean, you just stopped, Walter. I begged you to see someone—therapist, doctor, bartender. Get some help, get some meds, get out and get whatever you needed. I made the goddamn appointments for you, but you never went, did you?"

"Uh-uh."

"I talked to my mother, your mother and that little shit-heel wife of your brother's. Even she ran out of spiteful jabs after a while. Silver lining, right? I read books, I scoured the internet and now I...I don't know what else to do." She fought to contain an outburst of emotions *and fear and everything else Walter couldn't find within himself.*

She'd pretty much gathered herself together by the time they pulled up beside a little gate house. A man wearing a ranger hat leaned out.

"Mornin' ma'am," he drawled.

Angie fumbled bills out of her wallet, handed them over. "Is this where we go for the hiking trail?"

"Yes, ma'am. Visitor Center is just up on your right."

An elaborate shrubbery squatted in front of a single story building. Early enough still, no one much around. The parking area was mostly empty, but Angie didn't pull into a spot. She idled the car right out front. Looked over at Walter for what might've been the first time since they'd left Connecticut. Her puffy eyes were darkly wet and shiny.

"Okay," she said. "All this fresh air and exercise will...maybe help clear your head, give you a new perspective...."

Now that they'd arrived, he could see the heat of her resignation was quickly cooling. Would become a cold, sunken guilt deep in the pit of her soul before she made it out of the state. As much as anything else, he didn't want that. He opened his mouth, tried to say something.

Nothing came out.

"For a while there we were floating along with our head's up, babe," she said. "But now you've gone under. And with them around," she jerked her head at the backseat, at the two empty kiddie-seats belted there, "I can't let you take us all down. I can pick up more shifts. My parents will help. I don't want to, but I can go this alone. Without you dragging me down, I can maybe keep my head up or, or at least close enough."

Another pause, during which Walter understood the time for words had passed. It was time for him to go. Angie popped the trunk release.

Still, he couldn't make himself move until she sighed, unbelted and got out.

They met at the back of the car. She struggled to lift his backpack. Even working together, they made an ugly job of setting it on the curb. The pack whunked down with a certain hulking finality.

She put a small hand on his bicep, gripped it tight enough to leave a mark through layers of clothes. "This isn't me leaving you, Walter. Understand? Me and the kids are at home, we haven't gone anywhere. We're not going anywhere. It's you that's left us," she gestured around with her free hand at the Visitor Center, at the parking lot and finally at Walter's bedraggled self. "All this only makes it official."

She reached for his wallet. He stood by, listlessly watching her remove credit cards, bank cards, his AAA membership—everything that was linked to their joint finances. She returned the much depleted wallet to him with a thin white bank envelope.

"The plastic is pretty much melted already, but I...I sold your guitar."

Angie watched closely as Walter's mouth dropped, hung there loose on its hinges. She tensed, eager for protest, condemnation, anger: pretty much anything except the wet gurgle that came out.

"Thought that might get a bigger reaction," she said, not bothering to hide her disappointment. "And I'm sort of sorry, but you haven't played the stupid thing in years. Think I got a good price, but still, it's not much."

He stood there blankly. A silence stretched out between them like the lead rope on a snow-field traverse.

"It's gonna be an adventure," she finally said, painfully prolonging the scene. "I bet you meet lots of interesting people and...."

"Please, Angie," he finally croaked, "I really don't want—"

She leaned close, face contorting around a fierce whisper, "Don't you come back until then. If this doesn't work, go stay with your brother, set up under some bridge or just, I don't know...disappear. Don't you come

back to us all empty like this. Cuz that's what you are now—dried up
and empty like...like...."

Sometime during this speech, her bottom lip started up quivering.
Got so bad she couldn't finish the sentence. Just quick kissed him on
the cheek, turned and left him standing there.

Breathlessly numb, Walter watched Angie swing the car around.
Pulled up next to him, window already rolled down and tears falling
freely. "Good luck, babe," she managed, and then she was gone.

♣

To Bartleby, a quivering lip was *the* sign, the physical indica-
tor that Angie'd lost control of herself and, by extension, him
and all the downward spiraling bullshit of their life together.
Lot of things he'd have done to forestall even one lip quiver.
Hitching into a town he'd not planned on visiting was way
low on the list.

Bartleby cleared his throat, "So you gonna show me how to
do this?"

"Do what?"

"Hitchhike. I sorta never really, you know, hitchhiked
before either."

"Really?" Tortoise sniffled, "Figured I was the only person
out here who hasn't."

"Uh-uh."

"Well, so far all I know is it kinda sucks. Basically asking
total strangers for help, right?" She dropped her thumb, "And
holding your hand out gets pretty tiring after a while."

Bartleby shrugged, gestured down the road to the west,
"We going this way?"

"What is it with you guys?" Tortoise snapped. "Can't possibly believe a stupid girl can read the data book all by herself? Hiawassee is west of the AT. For northbounders, west is left. I'm not a complete retard, you know."

Bartleby nodded slowly, "I wasn't trying to second guess you. I'm not carrying a data book, trail guide or any maps, so pretty much for that reason and a handful of others, I *am* a complete retard."

"Sorry, I'm—" Tortoise shook her head, as if to clear it, "—well, I'm sorry."

They heard the next westbound car before they saw it.

"Go ahead, you give it a try," she said. "I'm jinxed."

He stuck a thumb out and stood facing eastward waiting for the car to come whipping down the pass. It was a Ford pick-up, a rusty old beater barreling along fast and loose. The driver braked hard and came to a rattling stop a little ways beyond them.

Tortoise squealed with delight. Bartleby moved towards the truck. Stalled and turned back. "Now what?"

"I don't know."

Fortunately for them, the driver had some experience with the process. An old woman with a wrinkled and sun-browned face rolled down her window, waved a cigarette at them. Bartleby hustled over. She blew a cloud of smoke out the window, "Where y'all headed?"

"West," he said, and quickly followed that with "Left" when the driver started to look confused. Finally, he pointed ahead to help clarify, "This way."

"Sorta figured as much. What's your destination?"

"I don't know." The thought hadn't crossed Bartleby's mind.

"Where are we going?" he called to Tortoise, who already had a leg up and over the tailgate.

"The Blueberry Patch."

The driver nodded, "Get in."

The truck was accelerating as half of Bartleby's bulk was still poised over the tailgate. It was a steady six or seven miles of big looping downhill curves. At the posted speed limits, the curves would've been gentle. As it went, they weren't gentle. That old Ford spent a good half the time straddling the yellow line.

Tortoise stole a glance in through the window, grinned nervously, "She's going like eighty."

Leaning there up against the tailgate, Bartleby nodded. Fifteen or a hundred and fifty, crash and burn, he didn't care, just as long as that damn bottom lip stopped quivering.

"Jus' saying. Coulda called me Booney. You know, cuz of the hat."

"Coulda."

"Or Ranger Rick. You know? Cuz I was an army ranger and my name's Rick and we're out here in the woods now."

"Didn't know any of that."

"Coulda asked. I got Ranger Rick a lot at Fort Benning. 'Cept it usually turned into Danger Dick. Jus' saying, didn't have to call me Skunkers."

"Beat you by sixty-two points. Where I come from, that's called getting double skunked. Somehow the name seemed appropriate."

"So? You got lucky cards is all."

"Uh-huh."

"And I got unlucky cards."

"Uh-huh."

"Only one game. Everybody knows one game don't mean nuttin'."

"Means something, *Skunkers*."

"Jus' saying."

The real stuff started coming down a mile short of the North Carolina border. Got cold and nasty, windy and wet real quick. The clouds had been darkening ominously for the last hour, but Bawdy hadn't expected much to come of it. He was wrong.

A pelting, piercing rain bored down upon his sparsely covered pate, his bare arms, his tired thighs. If it wasn't actually freezing out, it was close enough for him. He'd always had poor circulation and wasn't surprised to feel his hands going numb. To try and keep the blood moving he kept squeezing the handles of his hiking poles over and over.

He came upon a gnarly old tree over to his left. The guide book had something to say about the tree, made a big deal about it, but he couldn't remember exactly why. Nearer to trail, a short wooden sign was bolted to a different tree. The rain was playing havoc with his vision, fogging and flooding out his glasses, took him a bit to make out the simple block letters:

N.C./G.A.

Apparently Bawdy had reached his first state line. Another step or two and he'd walk out of Georgia and into North Carolina.

From the border, it was only another three miles to the next shelter. Course these three miles were all uphill. The wind brought a branch crashing down. Wasn't dangerously close or anything, but still got him to thinking about getting smushed and pinned under a couple tons of tree trunk. The trees overhead were all swaying and moaning. Lightning seamed the sky and was followed closely by tumbling thunder. He stooped low, as if this would somehow keep him safe.

"A tempestuous noise of thunder and lightning heard..." Bawdy recited, "Why, now blow wind, swell billow, and swim bark! The storm is up, and all is on the hazard...."

It wasn't too long before Bawdy came up on Old Man Trouble. Trouble was stopped dead in the middle of a steep climb and talking into a phone. He gave Bawdy a big friendly wave.

"What's the matter?" Bawdy asked. Had to shout to be heard over the wind and rain.

"What?"

"Are you okay?"

"Yeah," Old Man Trouble said, grinned and then his face dropped, "Are you? Is something wrong?"

"I'm fine." Screaming now, "What's happening?"

"Weather whipped up some, huh?"

"Are you on the phone?"

Old Man Trouble nodded distractedly, like maybe somehow he'd forgotten about the phone in his hand. "My wife. You wanna say hi?" Trouble handed the phone to Bawdy, who initially reached for it, but caught himself in time wave it off. Bawdy gave Trouble the glaring look he reserved for particularly thick students, "We gotta get to the shelter, I'm freezing!"

The trail was narrow enough that Bawdy had to step around Trouble, chest-to-chest. Climbed another thirty yards and looked back. Fog was so thick, he couldn't even make out the crazy old bastard's silhouette.

Bawdy made Muskrat Creek Shelter a bit after noon. Already six people were holed up inside. Bawdy couldn't feel his arms past his elbows and mostly wasn't feeling anything below mid-thigh. Got himself a spot in the shelter nestled between two people he'd never seen before. Pork Chop and Ella. Pork Chop was a big burly fellow with a scruffy red beard. To Bawdy's untrained eye, Pork Chop looked like a rough and tumble lumberjack. He wore a red and black checked wool shirt and spoke with a heavy Minnesotan accent. Even the 'chop' in his name seemed to suggest a past spent with an axe in hand.

Ella wasn't as easy to pigeonhole. She was a girlish woman, somewhere in her twenties he guessed. Even by Bawdy's not so stringent rubric, she was only sorta okay looking. Certainly better than he usually ended up with, but still not a looker by any objective metric. A freckly redhead with a button nose and four chubby cheeks. Two of which, at least, he could see were red with cold. She was only wearing silk-weight thermal tights and was pretty much popping out of them. He figured those two cheeks couldn't be much warmer.

Bawdy couldn't put a finger on it exactly but there was

definitely something off with Ella. Seemed like maybe some of her social wiring wasn't up to code, had maybe been left dangling by some unreliable contractor. Getting a spot next to a girl in a crowded shelter was suspicious. In his short time out on the AT, he'd already come to understand some of the natural dynamics of shelter life.

Generally, women were in short supply out in the woods. Specifically, and on a percentage basis, less of them overnighted in shelters than men. Shelters offered up less privacy and a hell of a lot more snoring. When women did shelter, he'd observed that men seemed to fill in around them pretty quick. Nothing but time to think while hiking, and he'd spent some of that thinking time concluding that there were probably some non-pervy benefits to this behavior. Usually women smelled better. They didn't necessarily smell good, but they smelled a hell of a lot better than most of the men. Also, on average, they tended to snore less. Not a hard and fast rule of course, but still a stereotype worth paying attention to. Lastly and probably least importantly, there was always the biologically driven directive, the slimmest consideration that maybe lying there next to a woman would lead to, well, lying next to a woman. Far as Bawdy could tell, this might've been a protective thing, something set instinctually deep in men. Or it could've been a 'getting some' thing. Half the time it seemed like the decision to sleep next to women in shelters wasn't even a conscious one.

So, he laid out his sleeping pad next to this Ella chick, and wormed into his mummy bag and warmed both himself and his suspicions.

Right off, Ella started talking down at him. Not questions, not conversation, and no kind of light banter—she dived right into her life story. Course, Bawdy quickly realized calling it a story wasn't precisely accurate. He'd come to understand during his decade spent in higher learning that, by definition, a story inherently comes with a beginning, a middle and an ending. This monologue of Ella's had no arc, no direction, no tension and no sign of ever concluding. She mentioned a master's degree from NYU. She had an annoying habit of using big words and immediately defining them, as if there was no way her audience could follow along without explanations. Took him three minutes to decide she was one of those people who come off as smart enough, but not nearly as smart as they think they are.

According to this rambling regurgitation, Ella's AT adventure was being entirely funded by solicited donations. She had browbeat local businesses and outdoor gear manufacturers for free gear and then she went and shook the branches of her family tree for pledges of support, starting at a penny a mile walked. Ostensibly she was raising money for breast cancer research, but she seemed a lot more interested in talking about all the freebies she'd wrangled. Her clothes were from Patagonia and her gear was top of the line.

"So, I'll be blogging about the hike. You know, putting out a daily multimedia diary type thing," she handed Bawdy a business card. It had her contact information with the web address of her blog on it. "Now you can follow along."

The absolute last thing Bawdy wanted to do was follow someone else's thru-hike on the internet but he dutifully tucked the card away. The whole thing sounded like a cheesy-ass scam to him, and possibly even more work than if she'd simply taken a side job and saved up for the hike like everyone else.

When Bawdy caught Pork Chop's eye, he found there a glint

of better-you-than-me bemusement, a wry flash of did-you-really-think-the-spot-next-to-the-kinda-cute-twenty-some-thing-chick-would've-been-available-if-she-wasn't-a-non-stop-nightmare?

Bawdy looked at the time, it wasn't quite one o'clock. He sighed and tucked himself down tighter into his sleeping bag while Ella droned on and on.

♣

There were already eleven people crowded into the shelter when Coyote arrived with Old Man Trouble in tow. Both of them were soaked through and shivering enough to lose teeth. Coyote's hair was all slicked down and back, made his face look unfortunately sharp and weasely.

"Any room left for a coupla hypothermic hikers?" With all the wet clothes, the dripping pack covers and the assorted gear hanging down from the low rafters, the place looked packed up and stuffed full.

"I'm not staying," Old Man Trouble said, "I just need to sign the register and I'm moving on." He shivered and took a pull from a little plastic hip flask.

"Are you crazy?" Bawdy asked. "It's hailing out there and you're wearing a cotton t-shirt."

"Sleeting," Pork Chop corrected.

"What?"

"It's not hailing. Hail is frozen snow. Sleet is freezing rain. It's sleeting out there."

"How about, it's cold as shit and the old guy's nothing but elbows and earlobes," Bawdy said. "He's gonna die."

"Listen," Old Man Trouble said, his eyes and face flush with mock seriousness, "I'm seventy-two years old. I eat what I want. I drink what I want. I hike big miles and I still have lots of sex. No way is a little hail gonna kill—"

"Sleet," Pork Chop corrected.

"I don't care if we're up to our asses in ooblek—there's lots of daylight left."

"It's like deep dusk out there," Pork Chop whispered to Bawdy.

"Alright already," Coyote cut in, "here's the register. Beat it, would ya?" He ran a hand through his wet hair, gave the shelter occupants a hungry leer, "You guys gonna make space for one more?"

An embarrassed pall settled on the shelter's occupants. No one wanted to say there wasn't room, but no one wanted to spend the next eighteen hours squeezed any tighter than they had to. And where would it stop—if twelve people could fit into the eight-man shelter, why not thirteen or fourteen or twenty even?

Finally Ella asked, "Don't you have a tent?"

"Sure I've got a tent. But if you think I want to go set it up in this, you ought to get yourself a check-up from the neck up."

The silence resumed.

"Alright, you bloodsuckers." Coyote pulled a wad of money from his pack. A single thick rubber band gave the wad a vague rounded shape, like a worn, old baseball. He thumbed a bill off the top. "I got a hundred bucks for the person that gives me their spot."

Only response was rain beating down on the roof.

"Tough crowd, huh?" He rooted through his pack again,

came up with a deck of cards, "Okay, here's the deal. I'll put up a hundred bucks *and* we cut for it. I win, I get your spot, you get the hundo. I lose, you keep your spot *and* the hundo. And that's the best deal any of you donks are getting today."

"Mac and cheese," Pork Chop said.

"What's that now?"

"Throw in a mac and cheese and I'll cut with you."

Coyote beamed his slickest grin at Pork Chop.

❧

"Can you believe the guy had me on the phone with his wife?" Coyote chuckled. He laid there next to Bawdy in his red sleeping bag looking more than a little like a jalapeno pepper. "I got lightning cracking, trees creaking, branches falling—the wrath of god coming down all around, I can't feel my ears, I'm out of breath. I'm actually starting to get a little scared, you know? And she wants to know if I think he's getting enough greens in his diet. Asked about his skin color."

The interior of the shelter was already shadowy and those shadows were stretching towards dark. A few people were still trickling in, though the flow of new arrivals had tapered off significantly in the last hour. When Bawdy last braved the elements and mad-dashed to the privy, he'd counted twenty-two tents and tarps pitched in the surrounding area. Was hardly any decent tenting to begin with, and now the only remotely flat patches of ground were brimming with rain water and mud. The privy trail was sloppy saturated and churned up like a dirt road come the spring thaw. Twice he'd had to stop and recover one of his Crocs from a particularly sucky mud hole.

The final count was twelve people sleeping on the shelter platform. From left to right: Giggles, Tommy Hawk, Walking Proud, Hungry Joe, Ella, Bawdy, Coyote, Jersey George, Quick Time, Going Good and this goofball teen named Pizza. They were shoe-horned in tight—cheek-to-jowl, shoulder-to-shoulder, head-to-toe and butt-to-gut. Sleeping pads were overlapped like so many mahjong tiles. Everyone got to know their neighbors pretty quick. When Hungry Joe coughed over on the other side of Ella, Bawdy could feel it. Get up to take a whiz and you stepped on three people, minimum. Going Good held the current record. In returning from the privy he somehow bungled it and fell from Quick Time all the way across to Walking Proud, spilled Hungry Joe's bowl of ramen and gave Jersey George a charlie horse.

The twelfth person, High-Ku, was laying crosswise down at the platform's edge. He was pretty much playing the role of doormat, but considering he wasn't carrying any kind of tent, he was happy for the part. A traveling beatnik who smelled like he'd been pickled in patchouli oil, High-Ku considered himself a pot-smoking poet of some caliber. True to his name, he penned an original haiku in the register each night and, task completed, promptly one-hit himself to sleep.

"Is that you cutting the cheese?" Coyote whispered to Bawdy.

"Uh-uh."

"Okay, I don't know who keeps dropping butt-bombs," Coyote yipped at his fellow shelter-mates, "but you gotta knock it off. I got this gag reflex thing—keep it up and I'm gonna paint this shelter in puke."

✤

"I'm cold," Bawdy said to himself as much as anyone else. There had been a warming up period, but that was hours ago now. Had on every stitch of dry clothing he possessed, but still the tingling toes were on their way back to numb and it wasn't quite seven o'clock. He'd already eaten two and a half meals, drank a pot of cocoa and a pot of tea. Had learned a new knot from Tommy Hawk, played a stirring round of jacks with Pizza and High-Ku, had even been subjected to Ella's political views, the ins and outs of her sibling relationships and just a few of her hopes for the future.

"I'm hungry," Pizza said.

"I'm bored," said Coyote, "and I miss the Blueberry Patch. Tell me again why we didn't hostel it for another day?"

Bawdy snorted, "Because *you* didn't want to lose Flutterby."

"Well, excuse me for trying to serve myself a nice slice of Flubby Pie. Where'd she get to anyway?"

"I don't know. Somewhere out there. Can't imagine it'll be any fun sleeping in that little hammock of hers, huh?"

"Just looking at that thing makes me seasick." Coyote shuddered. "Well, we *really* should've crammed a few more pancakes in this morning.

"You had seventeen."

"They were little and why were you counting?"

"Wanted to make sure I ate more than you did," Bawdy said.

"And?"

"Nineteen."

✤

Bawdy was just about halfway through *Slaughterhouse-Five*.

"Is that good?" Ella asked. "I've always wanted to read it."

"Sure, yeah, it's a classic." She put her hand out for him to hand over the book.

"Think I'd like it?"

"I really don't know, Ella. It's funny. You're welcome to borrow it when I'm—"

"This the page you're on?"

"Yeah."

RRRRIIIIPPPPPPPPPPPPPP

Ella returned the second half of the book to Bawdy and smiled, "Thanks."

In his entire life, Bawdy had not once considered tearing a book apart. He didn't dog ear them, he didn't leave them lying open, he didn't jam them into the bottom of a suitcase where they could get roughed up. Mostly he read them and tucked them safely away on high shelves, like hallowed artifacts. As he watched her rip his book in half, it felt like a piece of his soul was being torn asunder. Other than some shocked stammering, he couldn't even begin to voice his anguish.

❦

The rain stopped sometime in the wee hours, but the cold kept right on. Bawdy had come to the realization that cold was a bit like hunger, in that it was similarly tough to sleep through. Ella must've been feeling it too because she'd wiggled her way over, backed it right up and was spooned in tight against him.

He'd shift away, an inch or so, just to break contact, but ten minutes later, there she was, worming up against him again. Bawdy kept retreating until he was all but cuddled into Coyote's lap. He had Coyote nose-whistling in one ear, Ella purring in the other, various other sniffling-snorts rising up from the other shelter occupants, the wind still banshee-howling outside, twenty-one throbbing cold digits and an aching full bladder that he desperately didn't want to go out and empty.

❦

Bawdy woke to a stiff jab in the ribs. Must've gotten turned around in the night. When he opened his eyes, he was eyeball-to-eyeball with Coyote.

And Coyote was all googly-eyed and gesturing at something behind Bawdy. Bawdy fumbled his glasses into place and rolled over. Slanting morning sunlight illuminated the shelter. And back lit Ella. She was standing nearby, facing away and just starting to work her thermal tights down. She wasn't naked or anything, had little blue panties on under the tights, but it wasn't like they came close to covering all of her. What did actually cover all of her were freckles. And it wasn't some freckles, or even a lot of freckles. It was a galaxy's worth of freckles, innumerable red-dwarves, all of which, at least from Bawdy's perspective, could be linked together so as to make constellations of every shape and size. They spotted the back of her thighs and her flanks, blossomed upwards along the exposed cheeks of her ass, and higher still, above the blue panty waist. They continued on until disappearing beneath her waffled thermal fabric.

❦

Register: Muskrat Creek Shelter

4/12 Wet socks overhead
      make drip-splash lullabies, but
      will they ever dry?

                      High-Ku

4/12 LOST: middle-aged man, mopesy-dopesy, grunts a
           lot. May respond to Bartleby if called.
      IF FOUND: Please hurry his lazy ass north.
      REWARD: A backrub from Coyote Slick.

                    - Bawds

❧ ❧ ❧

For Bartleby, it was his biggest day of hiking so far. Yesterday, he'd come out of Hiawassee with a full pack and little ambition, ambled five miles and spent a listless night at Plumorchard Gap Shelter.

This morning, he'd gotten up and out like an early bird going for the worm. Spent the day lumbering along, alone and without many breaks. His feet must've really been on the mend because, even after nineteen miles, they weren't screaming for him to stop. According to the last trail sign it was only another mile or so to Carter Gap Shelter.

Though Bartleby was officially alone, he didn't much feel that way. Seemed like around every bend there were popcorn grasshoppers, lightning-fast lizards and more wild turkeys than he cared to count. Least once an hour he could hear a pileated woodpecker—pecking, pileating and otherwise going about its business up in some distant tree. Almost stepped on a baby snake, curled into a tight roll and sunning in the middle of trail. He did accidentally step on a yellow and black centipede-looking bug. Made a gooey mess of it too. At one point his simple presence was enough to stir up an unruly rabble of blue-bottomed butterflies. Was like walking through a kaleidoscope's fractured view of a brilliant cyan sky.

Time and distance both clicked past without his notice. Once he'd built up some steam, gotten a little momentum, warmed up and stretched out aching muscles, the conscious part of his mind was lulled to sleep by white blazes and rustling leaves. And heavy pack or no, he felt two tons lighter without laboring under the immediate burden of all those personal doubts and disappointments that his conscious mind couldn't help but chew over.

❧

When Bartleby arrived at Carter Gap Shelter, he immediately set to work cooking. Despite the simple design (little more than a cup with holes in the top), he still hadn't gotten the knack of his alcohol stove. It worked okay, he guessed, but certainly seemed to have a mind of its own. Sometimes it kicked blue flames eight, ten inches high, above the top of his pot. Or sometimes it would inexplicably snuff out. Took lots of cajoling and patience to bring a pot of water anywhere near a boil. Price was right though, and lukewarm, crunchy pasta was way better than nothing.

Bartleby, Blitz, Two-Speed Tortoise, Hairbrained, and Lazy JoJo were all circled around a fire when Pony Express staggered into camp.

Pony Express was forty something years old with a big soft body mushy as week old fruit. If possible, and in a nice way, he was softer inside than out. He arrived gasping and shambling, sweat-streaked, dirty, chewed up by the trail and all but spit out. The guy made Bartleby look like an old hand, a tough customer, a regular mountain man.

Pony Express didn't say two words. He dropped pack and plumped down near the fire with a regretful sigh.

Which was fine, because Blitz was asking Tortoise about her trail name. "Slow and slower, ja?"

She started to say something but Hairbrained beat her to it, "I wish. Try slowest and stopped."

Easy to tell by the way he said it, sort of hanging there after "stopped" with his eyes alight and his mouth still open, he expected an eruption of laughter. Wrong crowd for that. Tortoise's face dropped. Blitz was too busy translating the punch line, Pony Express was lost to the world and Bartleby wasn't even listening. Only Lazy JoJo managed anything close to laughter, a braying cackle that was itself much funnier than anything Hairbrained had said.

❦

It was nice not packing a tent around with him. Specially one as heavy and leaky as his had been. But there were nights when Bartleby wouldn't have minded the additional burden. This was one of those nights.

He could hear mice skittering along the shelter rafters, climbing walls and sniffing for crumbs. Rooting through gear and backpacks like they owned them. One particularly brave/ stupid mouse had gone so far as to clamber up and over the far end of Bartleby's sleeping bag. Its little feet scratching an easy purchase on the nylon material. He'd kicked his feet, catapulted the mouse across the shelter. It landed somewhere over by Pony Express.

A fusty and faintly acrid smell of stale urine clung to the shelter walls. Mouse pee wasn't really much different from cat pee in that regard. The lucky hikers got used to it, but it still wasn't any kind of solid foundation for a sound night's sleep.

The shelter platform was simply a hard wooden floor. It was worn smooth and oddly warped in places, but it had no give whatsoever. Bartleby preferred to sleep on his side which, without a decent pillow supporting his head and a mattress for his hip bone and shoulder to sink down into, was an unlikely prospect at best. He kept rolling over to relieve the aching pain in one shoulder only to roll again in twenty minutes to relieve the pain in the other. So it was mostly back sleeping and that meant serious snoring.

Which wouldn't have put Bartleby in any kind of minority. Could hear the occasional whuff-snort coming out of Blitz over the caustic tones of electro-techno leaking out of his ear buds. The new guy, Pony Express, had this slow and squeaky "meeeeeeeeeeeeeeeeeeeee" whine and Lazy JoJo, sleeping with that toothpick still in her mouth, well, she was in a class all by herself. She made lots of noises: wheezing-guffs, grumbling-wozzes, slurping-sighs and these sudden, explosive gnort-pooooos that echoed off the shelter walls.

Course, everyone else was having similar problems sleeping through the night. If someone wasn't snoring, they were likely rustling around, tossing, trying to find a sliver of comfort, getting up for a whiz or defending them and theirs from raids by the local rodent population.

Made him wish he'd taken an Ambien or two back when Bawdy had offered them.

❦

Register: Carter Gap Shelter

4/14 When I write the word TRAIL in my journal, at least half the time I spell TRIAL instead. Can't be a good sign......
                                                        Pony Express

❦ ❦ ❦

Coyote came up on a little clearing in the woods, a nice shaded spot with an enthusiastic spring blurgling through. Skunkers sat leaning against a tree trunk stabbing strips of jerky into a jar of peanut butter.

"Good spot for lunch, huh?"

"Meals kinda get confusing out here," Skunkers said. "I ate lunch hours ago. Had an afternoon snack like two miles back. Technically, this should be dinner, but it's way too early, right?"

"Whatever," Coyote grumbled, "I don't care so long as I'm eating," He hadn't snacked two miles ago and he was feeling light-headed and shaky. Snarfed two Twix bars almost without chewing. Chugged half a quart of water and started in on a bag of Fritos.

An acorn plopped down from an overhanging tree, landed

near Skunkers. He picked it up and absentmindedly tossed it at a rotten log some fifteen yards distant.

So then, of course, Coyote picked up an acorn and tossed *it* at the log. When his went closer than Skunkers' had, he pumped a fist and cheered, "Yahtzee!"

Skunkers quick threw another acorn. He pinged it off the log.

"That's nothing," Coyote said, "bet you a beer I can toss one into that knot hole before you do."

"You know I was—"

"A big bad army ranger. Yeah, you mention it twenty times a day. Only time you don't bring it up is when you're asleep, except with all the thrashing nightmares you pretty much bring it up then too. But really, what the hell has any of that got to do with throwing acorns?"

"—a varsity pitcher in high school. All four years."

"I have trouble believing that, Skunky."

"What? I don't look athletic?" Flexed an arm, "Get a look at this cannon."

"No, I can't believe you actually made it through four years of high school. Woulda guessed you faded away hours after turning sixteen."

"You're just tickling the tiger, Slick. Let's go—shot for shot. From where we sit. And the acorn's gotta stay in the hole. Don't count if it pops out."

Thru-hikers are a constant presence on the AT all year round, rain or shine. And when the weather isn't too bad the trail plays host to innumerable day hikers, weekenders and section hikers. Some section hikers come out year after year, inching along until they stitch together an entire thru-hike. Others come out with no bigger plan than to survive a few nights in the woods.

Thru-hiking purists call themselves white blazers. They progress along from white blaze to white blaze, not missing a single step of the trail. The myriad hiking paths that intersect and branch from the AT are blazed with blue paint to help distinguish them from the AT proper. Blue blazers are those hikers who take the occasional side trip or short cut. If a side trail seemed easier or shorter or just more interesting, a blue blazer would take it and miss a piece of the AT without regret.

As much as hiking, yellow blazers advance via hitches and bummed rides. Their name comes from the yellow lines in the middle of the road. Often prompted by time constraints, injuries or a waning interest in hiking, yellow blazers are known to hitch around difficult stretches or simply cherry pick the more appealing sections of trail. They like to bask in the glow of trail culture without any of the hard work.

When these white, blue or yellow blazers get tired of lugging gear, slackpacking is always an option. Slackpacking entails coordinating shuttle rides to and from trail so that a hiker can advance without carrying a fully loaded back. It's all about covering more ground with less effort.

It entails coordinating shuttle rides to and from trail, so that a hiker can advance without carrying a fully loaded backpack.

The white-blazing purists tend to look down on slackpackers, but this doesn't much bother them. They're moving way too fast to notice.

* * *

"I'll catch up," Pony Express called to Bartleby.

The rate he hiked, it was unlikely that he'd catch up until dinnertime, but that didn't matter. What Pony was really saying was, *I'll be pulling off into the woods now and getting down to some serious number two-type business in the very immediate future. It would be in our collective best interests for you to keep on meandering in a general northerly direction.*

Bartleby waved, kept on hiking and Pony Express veered off trail.

He'd been trying to hold on until the next shelter, but it was still three miles away and no way could he postpone things for another hour and a half.

And so Pony crunched through the low growth, scanning nervously for snakes and an appropriate spot to drop his drawers.

In a general sense, Pony was happy to be out hiking. Specifically, though, there weren't many aspects of thru-hiking that he actively enjoyed. Not yet, anyway. Everything was getting better, but progress was painfully slow. With an emphasis on painful.

Of the long list of unenjoyable pieces that made up the whole of his trail experience, pooping in the woods was easily the worst offender.

Back home Pony was old reliable, regular as a Swiss timepiece set to go off just after lunch. It was a refreshing moment amidst the hubbub of his day. He had twenty or so meditative minutes during which he would chuckle at a recent Harper's Index, feel sympathetically enlightened by a My Turn article or peruse the latest goings on in Shouts & Murmurs.

Within twenty-four hours of hitting trail, Pony's comfortable routine was ruined. Turned out excessive amounts of starchy food made him go; excessive walking made him go; even his pack belt, cinched tight around his middle, made him go.

And of course, the best of the privies didn't offer the same peaceful atmosphere to which he'd been accustomed. But that didn't actually matter much, because he generally had to go when there wasn't a privy for miles in any direction.

Some people popped off trail and, sixty seconds later, were already hoisting their pack back on. Pony had no idea how that was humanly possible. It sometimes took him five minutes to simply pick a decent spot. Picking a spot was no easy feat. He needed to go in far enough to be ensured of complete privacy, but not so far as to risk getting lost. Also, he was terribly frightened of snakes, and figured the more he tramped through the scrub-brush, the more likely he was to scare one up.

It was only after settling on a spot and digging a cat-hole with his orange pack trowel, that Pony hunkered down with shorts at his ankles and a certain determined mindset that he hoped would move things along expeditiously. Prolonged crouching sessions set his thighs on fire.

This time around, Pony was in luck, the master of his movement as it were. He was making good progress, expected to wrap things up expeditiously and in short order.

Except, somewhere ahead, the AT must've made a big lazy hook back on itself, because there was Bartleby, minding his own business and hiking along not twenty yards from where Pony was hunched over and hard at work.

"Gotta be almost there now, right? Can't be more than a mile. Right?"

"Dunno."

"Seriously? Been walking for days on end here."

"Dude, we left that last shelter like thirty minutes ago."

"Feels like forever." After carefully stone-stepping his way across a muddy patch of trail, Coyote started up again, "Okay, Skunky. I got one for ya."

"Got one what?"

"A bet."

"Yeah?"

"Give you a chance to win back that pint of ice cream you owe me. Double or nothing says I can name more presidents than you before we hit the next shelter."

"Seriously? Sucker. Washington."

Just before them the trail began to trend sharply uphill.

"And here it comes," Hairbrained said.

"Uh-huh," Tortoise said, leading the way.

Pony Express had a look of misgiving, "What?"

"Albert Mountain," she called back.

"Bad?"

Hairbrained grinned, "Short..."

"But?"

"Straight up. Supposed to be a fire tower up top too. Should be a cool view."

Bartleby sighed. Not carrying a data book was nice, you never knew what was coming next. Except that you never knew what was coming next.

And with that, the trail took off, gaining elevation with all the thrust and immediacy of a rocket launch. Streams of sweat fell from Bartleby as he scrabbled upwards, occasionally using his hands to pull himself forward. It was a ham hock burning, lung-bursting and pitiless climb, as near-vertical as a trail can get without becoming a climbing route. At first, Bartleby kept close on Tortoise's heels, but that didn't last long. Hairbrained stuck close behind Bartleby. He didn't try and pass even as Bartleby slowed to a more realistic pace and Tortoise pulled ahead. Got so Bartleby was resting every few steps to let the lactic acid burn subside and his lungs oxidize blood.

As advertised, the climb was short. When the worst of it was below him, Bartleby stood with hands on hips and his head swimming from the effort.

"Uhhhhh," was all Hairbrained could manage. Then, after minutes of heavy breathing, "Tortoise?"

Bartleby shrugged, "Musta went on ahead. Girl moves faster than any tortoise I ever heard of."

"Moment there it felt like I might cough up a bit of breakfast," Hairbrained admitted. He dropped his pack, "And you know what that means—Pony Express is a lock for vomit."

With the sun shining and sheltered from the wind, the temperature was close to balmy. The exposed rocks at the summit radiated a soothing warmth. Seated in a little rock niche, Bartleby laid his head back and closed his eyes. Zoned out. Not quite asleep, but not totally awake either.

"There he goes," Hairbrained chuckled. "Looks like breakfast and maybe some of last night's dinner. Priceless."

As Pony climbed the last bit, Hairbrained called down encouragements which, to Bartleby's ear, sounded a lot like thinly masked heckling.

"Looks like you still got some puke on your chin there, Pony."

At the summit, Pony slumped over and sucked wind. Looked comically pathetic, like a wet kitten.

Hairbrained started up the fire tower stairs. "One of you needs to come up and take a picture of me on top," he shouted back over his shoulder.

Pony snorted, "What's that—another eighty feet straight up?"

Bartleby nodded yes.

"You going up?"

Bartleby shook his head no.

"Well, I guess that guy can go pluck a duck then."

Bartleby and Pony were already fifty yards up trail before Hairbrained reached the fire tower's viewing platform.

❦

"Shhhh. Hold up." Pony Express cupped a hand to his ear, "Listen. You hear that?"

Bartleby heard what sounded to him like a distant tractor engine coughing to life.

When the noise stopped, Pony smiled like they'd just shared a special moment.

"Bonasa umbellus. Commonly known as the ruffed grouse,

107

or more commonly called the chicken-of-the-woods. That was a male doing a territorial display called drumming. Beating his wings fast enough to create a vacuum. Exactly like how a lightning bolt makes—"

"A vacuum," Bartleby cut in, "and thunder is actually the sound of air rushing back in to fill the void."

"Uh, yeah. You got it. The ruffed grouse isn't exotic or anything, but I still get a thrill. Course, I could listen to pigeons cooing and be happy."

Bartleby never asked, but Pony Express was a big birder. Could recognize hundreds of calls and give a fair imitation of maybe half as many. Walking postal routes for twenty years gave him plenty of time for practice.

❧ ❧ ❧

Register: Big Spring Shelter

4/13 The "not-so" wily Coyote challenged me to name more presidents than him. Poor guy never heard of an old marching song called "The Presidential Parade." I started at Washington and marched straight through to a free pint of Ben & Jerry's.

Hoorah! Skunkers

❧ ❧ ❧

This wasn't Old Man Trouble's first time around the track. He went all the way thru to Maine back in '91—sort of a fiftieth birthday present to himself. Had such a fine time he decided to run it right back for his sixtieth in '01. And now again in '11—well, he had started a tradition, hadn't he? Sure his joints felt rustier and his muscles sounded creakier than he remembered, but he was still optimistic. With a little luck he'd go all the way thru this time too, score himself a hat trick of sorts, a poor man's triple crown. But if that didn't work out, he wasn't going to cry a river. The further the better, but really it was just nice to get back out in the woods and plug into the so-simple thru-hiking lifestyle. Trouble particularly enjoyed the smorgasbord that passed for community out here. Where else could a seventy-year old get to flirt with a girl like Flutterby, out-hike young whippersnappers or sit up on the summit of a little mountaintop all by his lonesome, smoke dope and listen to the wind's lonely song? If anybody could've answered that question and suggested a destination, he would've made a beeline there straight from the top of Katahdin.

Trouble had actually hiked around Poohbah for a while back during his '01 hike. Good lord, was that kid wound tight. Tough listening to him back then, and if possible, he was less tolerable this time around. Trouble staunchly believed that the trail provides for hikers, but it was like the poor little grump was desperately searching for something that just couldn't be found.

Far as Trouble figured it, the trick to thru-hiking, and hell, maybe life too, was not thinking about it all very much. Just keep stepping one boot in front of the other. You start doing the math, planning out how many miles, how many hours, how many mountaintops between you and the next town, the next state, or trail's end—well, that could quickly overwhelm a person. The tough truth of it was, there were thousands of miles, hundreds of long painful hours and many million tons of mountain standing between Springer and Katahdin. Best to put it out of mind and get on with what's directly ahead of you. Easiest way to do that was by engaging with your immediate surroundings. Enjoy the company of people you'd never have crossed paths with back in the "real" world, connect with the steady rhythms and intricacies of the natural world or just flat out laugh as much as you could.

🍁 🍁 🍁

Register: Rock Gap Shelter

4/15 Saw my first snake today. IN A TREE! Who knew they could climb?? I woulda peed myself for sure if I hadn't already been peeing.
                          Two-Speed Tortoise

🍁 🍁 🍁

Skunkers stopped dead and signaled for Coyote to do the same. Then he sniffed the air and made a show of studying the ground for footprints.

Coyote felt a little like he'd been thrust into a scene from a jungle war movie. He looked furtively around the woods and started to wonder if they were about to be eaten or if this was the beginning of a Deliverance-esque interlude with some backwoods locals. Either way, he was glad for that big serrated lock-blade knife Skunkers kept strapped to his pack. The thing looked badass. When Coyote couldn't take the silence anymore, he finally whispered, "What's the matter?"

Skunkers made some hand signals which Coyote couldn't pretend to understand.

He wanted to ask more questions, but thought better of it.

They started moving again, but quietly, purposefully, stealthily.

When they reached a fork in the trail some hundred yards later, a routered wooden sign explained that the blue-blazed side trail led point-four to a trailhead parking area. Skunkers started up sniffing again.

Coyote tried too, but he couldn't smell a thing, "What is it?"

"Someone's grilling cheeseburgers down in the parking lot."

"Cheeseburgers?"

"Barkers too."

"Barkers?"

"Hot dogs. Hebrew National, I think."

Skunkers set off loping down the side trail.

"Where you going?"

"Gonna go beg some burgers. Come on."

"You're crazy," Coyote shook his head, "I don't smell nothing."

Skunkers put a finger to his nose, "Trust me, Slick. I got a good sniffer."

"Do I look like a blue-blazer? I'm not wandering off trail, chasing after phantom cheeseburgers—"

"Guess you gotta hike your own hike, Slick." Skunkers shrugged, turned and set off down the side trail at a gallop.

❦

111

"Where's Skunks?" Bawdy asked when Coyote reached the shelter.

Coyote rolled his eyes, "Big Boy went off chasing cheeseburgers. Not gonna see him any time soon."

❧

This wasn't the first time that Skunkers' nose had led him astray. The hot dogs were Ballpark, not Hebrew National. Of course, smothered under spicy coleslaw as they were, it didn't much matter.

❧ ❧ ❧

Bartleby woke to the whoopee-cushion whoosh of Lazy JoJo deflating her Therm-a-Rest. He yawned, stretched and immediately set to tucking his sleeping bag into his pack. Next went excess clothing, his jacket, cook stuff and food bag. A water bottle into each of the side pouches. He stuffed toilet paper, headlamp and snack foods into his top pocket. When he'd jammed the last bits of gear away, Bartleby strapped his sleeping pad crosswise on the outside. Turned a tight circle, looking high and low; checking that he wasn't leaving anything behind. No socks left hanging to dry or a granola bar tumbled free from a half-zipped pocket. Had so few possessions now and they all played such vital roles in his day-to-day existence that leaving something behind was, at best, a colossal pain in the ass.

Out front of the shelter a dozen hikers were taking care of their various morning chores: cooking breakfast, collecting water, packing and generally readying themselves for another day of northbounding. The sun was well up over the horizon and the day was promising to be pleasingly bright and probably warm too.

Leaving his pack on the shelter platform, Bartleby minced barefoot over to an empty seat at the table and sat next to Pony who was recounting in excruciating detail some late-night mouse attack that he'd only just survived.

Bartleby knocked dirt from his feet. Kneaded his thumbs into aching arches, massaged heels, rolled ankles, cracked scabby toes. Best as he could, he inspected each foot—top, bottom and in-between all the little piggies. Dabbed antibiotic ointment where appropriate. He wore two pairs of socks, silken liners under thicker woolies. Yesterday's foot sweat had long dried but the socks were still unavoidably filthy. He gave each a vigorous whack against the table's edge, sending up plumes of dried dirt and dead skin.

After pulling the socks into place, he thumped his sneakers together. Turned them over, shook out any debris. The top of one sneaker had a nickel-sized hole in the webbing. Residual evidence left by a sharp stick that he'd impaled himself on while dashing off trail to take care of business. Brown-blazing someone had called it. Since then, the hole had been growing steadily. Now he could clearly make out the color of his sock through the thinned mesh. The sole on his other sneaker was beginning to peel away in the front. The treads of both sneakers had largely been worn down and the laces consisted more of knots than anything else. Had become difficult, if not impossible, to really tie them tight anymore.

Bartleby started on a Baby Ruth bar, stuffed a few other bars into his pocket for later, shouldered his pack and headed off up the trail.

* * *

A rag-tag looking dude came crashing out of the woods waving at Bawdy and Tommy Hawk with one hand while holding up his pants with the other. He had that underfed, greasy-haired, dirty-legged look of a thru-hiker, but no backpack in sight.

When he reached trail a little ways ahead of them, he waited there, bent over and breathing hard.

"Hey," he gasped, "I'm Squirtz."

"Hey."

"You guys hiking?"

Bawdy couldn't help himself and gave the guy one of his famously scornful now-isn't-that-about-the-stupidest-question looks before he could stop himself.

"Think maybe one of you could spot me—you know, lemme borrow some...toilet paper?"

Tommy Hawk shook his head. He wore a vaguely disapproving and entirely stern-faced frown, "Sorry, son. I'm regular like clockwork and have budgeted accordingly. I'm not packing one extra sheet and if I was I might give it to you, but I certainly wouldn't let you borrow it."

Squirtz looked at Bawdy, a certain hapless desperation evident in his eyes. "Don't make me use the leaves again, man. I don't wanna use the leaves."

Bawdy sighed, "Guess I could spare a little." Produced a ziploc full of toilet paper from one of his pack pockets. Squirtz took it, gave it the once over.

"Don't ya got any wipes?"

"Nope."

"Dude—everybody carries wipes."

Bawdy sighed, rolled his eyes and otherwise stalled. Squirtz patiently stood waiting. Bawdy gave up the bluff with an annoyed shake of his head and produced a yellow travel pack of wet wipes.

Squirtz swiped the wipes and bounded back into the woods, graceful and quick as a yearling deer.

It was pretty much two scoops to one. Over the last few "shared" meals, Two-Speed Tortoise had been counting while she chewed, swallowed and scooped quick as she could. But no matter how fast Tortoise ate, Hairbrained ate faster. At least twice as fast. And that meant he was eating twice as much.

To save weight he'd decided they would only carry one pot and cook a common meal each night. Initially that had sounded fine, but now she understood how lopsided that arrangement was. Instead of them each eating half, he wolfed down two-thirds of whatever they cooked and she was lucky to wrangle the remaining third for herself.

And that was with an even playing field. Sometimes the food was so hot she couldn't tolerate a single spoonful, and there he was chomping it away like a hungry, hungry hippo.

"Seriously, you've already eaten your half," she said. He grinned and went in for another scoop. "Brian, I'm not kidding, *you're* eating *my* dinner."

Scoop.

"Come on," he said, almost choking on a mouthful of rice, "I'm bigger than you, I need more calories to keep going."

Scoop.

"I hike as many miles and the way you keep sneaking stuff into my pack, I wouldn't be surprised if I'm carrying more weight than you by now too."

Scoop.

"Doesn't matter, I'm still bigger."

Scoop.

"It does matter. I go to bed hungry cuz you're eating my food! I carried it, I want to eat it. You need more food, carry more food. Don't eat mine."

Scoop.

🍁 🍁 🍁

"What was that noise?" Bawdy needed to know.

Flutterby was removing gear from her pack. "What noise?"

Bawdy hobbled over, stiff-legged and hip-sore, to where Flutterby was setting up her hammock. He scooped up a stuff sack she had recently put down and shook it to reproduce the aforementioned noise. A plasticy clatter-shake. "This noise, Missy."

He opened the stuff sack and pulled out a smaller bag. His face was illuminated with a certain interior light that usually only flickered on when he was reading. His voice went low, almost reverent, "Flubby Pie—why didn't you tell me you were carrying travel Scrabble?"

✤

Flutterby was carrying travel Scrabble. Had been since Amicalola Falls. Back before they married, her ex-husband had introduced her to the game. He was hardcore; a first degree tile maniac and an ecstatic Scrabble-onian. It was the one facet of her marriage that she cared to think back on with anything close to fondness.

Sure, she had played it with her grandmothers when she was younger, but not for real, not competitively.

Because Scrabble was important to him, it quickly became important to Flutterby. She studied, memorized the two-letter words, learned most of the three-letter words. It turned out she had some game. They played and challenged and bingoed together with a vivacity and energy that, looking back now, she understood was lacking from every other aspect of their relationship.

When she beat Bawdy 414 to 354, she shrugged it off, "I got good tiles."

"I could kiss you," he said. "I haven't lost a game of Scrabble in six years. And you can bet it wasn't to any kind of divine wood nymph such as yourself. I *cannot* believe you're carrying Scrabble on the AT."

"Well, considering how I just wiped your ass across the table here, Bawdy-boy, it seems like maybe you should be carrying the game. At least, you know, until you win one."

✤ ✤ ✤

"Give it up, Coyote."

"Come on—it's not so bad. More mysterious than anything else."

"It's the exact opposite of mysterious."

"Nah-uh. Sets me to wondering. "

"Well, stop wondering—I'm not taking it."

"You got a better idea? 'Ella' isn't cutting it. Not if you wanna make it to Maine."

"Course I'm making it to Maine. What's that got—"

"Then you need yourself an honest trail name."

"Why?"

"I read that people are way more likely to go off trail if they don't have a genuine trail name. You get a trail name, you feel connected out here and you're like four times more likely to reach Katahdin."

"Where'd you read that?"

"I don't know. Doesn't matter."

"You're lying."

"Sort of a big risk to take, isn't it?"

"Could just call myself Moon Moth or, I don't know...Walking Strong."

"Personally, I've already met a Strong Walker, a Long Walker, a Fast Walker, and a Walking Proud. You really wanna cram into that clown car?

"It seems like we're all out here to get away from our pasts and change our futures. Don't you figure a trail name is a fundamental part of that transformation? A new you needs a new name. Something unique, something personal, something with a little pizzazz. Some random name with no weight *behind* it—pun intended—well, how's that gonna help keep you on trail?"

"I'm done talking about this."

"Alright. Just say you'll think about it, okay, Frecklebutt?"

When Bartleby hit US-64, Lazy JoJo was standing on the shoulder with her thumb out, trying to flag down a ride.

"Going into Franklin?" she asked.

"Uh-uh. Still got plenty of food."

"Well, stand here and stick your thumb out anyway—I gotta piss like a plow horse."

Lazy JoJo squatted behind a bush.

"Been waiting thirty minutes so far," she called. "Don't know why people keep saying women have an easier time hitching."

Register: Siler Bald Shelter

4/16 Hitched a ride back to trail from Franklin on the short bus. Had real live tards—drooling, moaning and crapping themselves. The driver was an old dead-head, tried to sell us weed. Classic.

Coyote Slick

P.S. as we got off the driver told Skunkers to buckle back up.

P.P.S. worst shelter yet. Why'd I walk .5 off trail to have lunch at this rat box?

4/16 CLARIFICATION = the driver stopped me cuz
my PEZ dispenser fell outta my pack. Not cuz he
thought I was trying to escape.

Skunkers

4/16 To further clarify, a PEZ dispenser is dead weight.
Anyone stupid enough to carry one of those belongs
on a short bus. Slicker

4/16 Says you. I like PEZ. Skunks

4/16 Fine, but you don't need to carry the dispenser.
Slickest

4/16 But PEZ don't taste right if it ain't popping out of
some little dude's head. Skunky

4/16 Sometimes it feels like I'm stuck in one of those
special villages that got not just one, but two idiots.
—Bawdy

🍁 🍁 🍁

Just up and over Wayah Bald, past the squat stone tower on
the summit, early evening was settling in at Wayah Shelter.

"No bear cables here," Skunkers said.

"Seriously? Shit."

"You got rope? I sent mine home from Hiawassee. Hadn't
used it once."

Bawdy shook his head, called over to Coyote, "Hey, you got

any rope? No cables—we gotta hang our own bear bags tonight."

Coyote was setting up his tent, "How do you not have rope in that pack of yours, Skunkers? Figured you'd have enough to rig a ship." Coyote produced a loop of paracord out of his pack. "Listen, I got forty-five feet of p-cord. Which I will always carry and you can always borrow, but I never want to have to be involved with actually hanging the food. Deal?"

Bawdy balked. He'd read extensively on the topic, studied bear-bagging theory, memorized the different relevant knots and diagrams, but he'd never actually hung food up in a tree.

"Deal," Skunkers said.

"And no matter what, if she wants on, there is always room for Flubby's food."

"Sure, okay," Bawdy finally managed.

Skunkers took the p-cord and marched off into the woods. Only stopped long enough to make sure Bawdy was coming with.

"You know anything about any of this, Bawds?"

"I know everything about it, but..."

"But you've never actually hung food in a tree before."

"Uh-uh."

"Okay," Skunkers said through that easy smile of his, "we'll play to our strengths. You're the mastermind, I'm the muscle and Coyote, well I guess he's going to be the mule. That sound about right?"

❧

Despite all the advances in personal electronics—iPods,

e-readers, laptops, digital cameras, smartphones—and all the promise of entertainment these devices implied, bear-bagging was still, far and away, the single-most consistent source of amusement up and down the whole length of the Appalachian Trail.

Simply put, the objective of bear-bagging is the suspension of one's foodstuffs so that they are inaccessible to the various voracious denizens of the wilderness. On the East Coast, black bears can grow to six feet tall and five hundred pounds. Being agile climbers and omnivorous scavengers, it is necessary to suspend food at least twelve feet from the ground and ten feet away from any vertical supports from which the bears may reach over. There are various methods by which this can be accomplished. But ultimately, every method requires a rope be thrown over a high tree branch. Which is where the entertainment begins.

✤

"You got that knot tied tight?"

"Yep."

"Okay, I'm thinking that branch up there."

"The knobby one?"

"No. Go left a tree and a half. The branch with the leaf cluster that looks like a clown face."

"Half a tree?"

"Throw the rope already."

"Okay. Gimme some room."

Skunkers cocked back and hurled the stick/rope with good speed and height. Looked like it might actually loop over the intended branch, but for Bawdy standing on the line. When the loose cord played out, the stick jerked short and dropped to the ground.

"You're on the line, man."

"Yeah, sorry. Shit. Let her rip."

The stick went soaring up and over the target branch. Of course, without Bawdy anchoring the rope's free end, the stick and string just kept going up and completely over the branch. Landed in a heap thirty yards away.

"Maybe if I just hold the end," Bawdy suggested. Skunkers gave him a dark look.

Like the previous two, the third throw was right on target. Good height, plenty of distance and a healthy trajectory. A little too much oomph though. After the stick cleared the branch and the line pulled taut, the stick swung down and somehow looped around the branch twice and tangled itself stuck.

"Can you pull that back down?"

"I'm pulling. It's not coming. It's all grappled up."

"Sunnova bitch. Here, let me help."

And there ensued a few moments of serious exertion. Two full-grown men straining at the traces with their backs bent. Skunkers' arms bulged and Bawdy's face flushed. Finally, the stick broke and both halves fell to the ground. Without the stick gumming things up, the rope slipped free and puddled at their feet.

"Okay, we need a bigger stick."

They found a bigger stick. To which Bawdy affixed the p-cord. Skunkers threw it at the branch. They watched an un-tethered stick spin off into the woods.

"What happened?"

"The knot came undone."

"What knot did you use?"

"I don't know its name."

"What did it look like?"

"I wound the line around the stick and then tucked it back under."

"Yeah, that one doesn't have a name. You know why?"

"Why?"

"Cuz that's not a knot; that's nothing; that's just rope and a stick."

They found another stick. This time, Skunkers secured the rope with an anchor bend hitch he had learned in the Army. His next throw missed the branch wide. After that he missed the branch short, missed wide, somehow missed long, and then missed wide again. In fact, that last throw went so wide, it looped over a totally different branch.

"What'd'ya think, Bawds?"

Bawdy looked back at the shelter. At first it had just been Coyote and Flutterby watching, but now Ella and a handful of others were raptly following their bumbling efforts. Big grins a-beaming. No one wanted to miss a second of the action. "I think we look like a coupla flipping fools."

Skunkers ignored the onlookers, "Yeah, but can we hang food on that branch?"

"Well, if we do, our food's going to be in easy reach of that trunk. Be better if you could get the line over the first branch."

They got lucky pulling the line down. It almost snagged again.

After six more throws, Skunkers needed a breather.

"I think you're actually getting worse."

"Feel free to give it a go, bro."

Bawdy loosed a granny-style pop fly that went up and came straight back down, like an elevator. Nearly knocked his glasses off.

"*Gaaa.*"

"Fuck, dude."

Bawdy brushed himself off, handed the rope back to Skunkers, "Okay, how about that branch. The one standing out like a broken leg."

"I dunno. Looks higher."

"Maybe we'll get lucky.

Up and over on the first throw.

"Nice, Skunks."

They bumped knucks. They high-fived. They slapped backs and smiled big.

"You two are doing it wrong," Tommy Hawk told them. He'd come over to help. Tommy Hawk was retired military, but he still had the flattop. Even out in the woods, he made sure to shave every morning. Had been a major or colonel, but he carried himself like he had a couple of stars on his chest. Had an actual working tomahawk stuck through a belt loop. "Here," he said, "I'll show you how to do it."

"We just got it."

Tommy Hawk looked up at the branch with a disapproving sneer on his face, "Yeah? What method is that?"

"Throw the rope over a high branch," Bawdy said. "I call it Old Faithful."

Tommy Hawk shook his head, sighed and jerked the line down out of the tree. "I like to use the PCT method, so," he turned to Skunkers, "why don't you go ahead and see if you can round us up another line and a carabiner, son."

＊　＊　＊

After surviving a few weeks on trail, Bartleby was mostly over the learning curve.

It helped that his gear was simple. Didn't take any genius to operate an alcohol stove. He had no tent to fuss with. For him, water purification simply entailed counting out fourteen drops of Aquamira into a quart-sized bottle of water and waiting fifteen minutes. Without owning a guide book, he couldn't even spend hours worrying over it, plotting the next day's advance. Each morning Bartleby packed his few belongings and shambled northward. He ate the occasional meal and stopped for the night when he reached a likely looking shelter.

It helped that he didn't expect much. Many hikers spent months planning and preparing their thru-hikes and had, over that time, built up romantic expectations. The hike would be easy breezy, painless, meditatively quiet, quick, warm, dry and otherwise perfect; sometimes they imagined that stepping both feet on trail would somehow instantly make them different, better, whole. When these unrealistic hopes weren't met, more than a few hikers grew disillusioned, disappointed and discouraged to the point of quitting.

Bartleby started off disillusioned, disappointed and discouraged. He had no hope. He'd quit on life more than a year before setting one foot in Amicalola's parking lot. Hiking the Appalachian Trail hadn't loomed on Bartleby's horizon and he certainly didn't expect any miracles to come from it.

It helped that trail life was so straightforward and streamlined. Out in the woods, the mire of bullshit with which middle-class American suburbanites fill their lives became wholly unnecessary. There were no monthly electric bills, no television shows to keep up on, no kids to get off to school, no douche-bag boss to keep happy, no weekend plans to make, break or endure. To thru-hike meant to pass a summer without mowing lawns, whacking weeds or watering gardens. There was no sifting through the daily barrage of junk mail, no struggling to recall logins and passwords, no vacuuming soggy pretzels from under the kid's car seats, no family drama, and no creditors calling day and night.

Life on trail was physically demanding, but it certainly wasn't complex or jammed full with meaningless minutia. Really couldn't have been simpler. Drink water, eat food, walk miles. Turned out, Bartleby did each of these well enough to keep on keepin' on.

"Skunk," Bawdy called. If anyone had been really listening, they might've noticed a certain desperate tremor in his voice.

"He's off shining the moon," Coyote said. He was in his tent, hiding out from the relentless mosquitoes.

It wasn't quite dusk yet, but already Flutterby was laying and swaying in her hammock. Not trying to sleep exactly, but it had been a long day of hiking and it felt good to put her feet up. Despite having started before anyone else, Tommy Hawk was still busy staking out his tent. He tackled the task with a painstaking exactitude that would have shamed many a German engineer.

"Skunk," Bawdy repeated as he scurried past Coyote's tent.

"I already told you, he's taking a dump, dropping a deuce—" Coyote stopped mid-sentence. He suddenly found himself nose to nose with a skunk. Not Skunkers, but a real deal, black and white, stink spraying, bread box-sized naturally occurring bio-hazard. Nothing more than a single layer of bug mesh and six inches of fresh air between them.

It was an ugly stinker too, with a long, pinched face and lots of needly teeth. Dirty racing stripes started at each temple and swept back along the shaggy black fur of its flanks.

"Nobody move," Tommy Hawk said with all the practiced authority of his rank.

Coyote cringed back. He started up mumbling "I don't wanna get sprayed, I don't wanna get sprayed."

The skunk's shiny black eyes studied Coyote. Then it turned and sunk its teeth into his shoe. Got a good grip on the toe box and gave it a spine-snapping shake.

"*Somebody* do *something*," Coyote whisper-hissed.

Bawdy cowered behind one of the tree trunks supporting Flutterby's hammock, "What do we do, Tommy?"

"Stay still. Be calm. Don't scare it. It should go away if...."

"If what?"

"It's not rabid."

Flutterby's camera was easily accessible in the cargo pocket of her shorts. She slid it free.

"That can't be a good idea," Bawdy whispered.

Flutterby thumbed the zoom and snapped a picture. The skunk didn't much like the flash. It performed an awkward little jump-turn maneuver and took off speed waddling; disappeared nose-first under Tommy Hawk's tent.

For one moment the tent was stock still. Then it began to

bulge and flap and tremble in a way that Bawdy would later describe as cartoonish.

With his own tent suddenly at risk, Tommy Hawk's early composure collapsed with a rapidity that would've made Bear Stearns look like a malingerer.

"I'll kill your mother, you stinky rat fucker!" He followed this threat with ear-splitting blasts on the emergency whistle he kept hanging alongside his dog-tags. Kicked up tent stakes and freed guy lines until he could swing the tent aside like a matador's cape. Abruptly exposed again, the skunk cast around blindly and wrinkled its nose.

Before Tommy could fumble his tomahawk free, Flutterby snapped another picture. The skunk took off crashing through leaf litter and scampering southward along the AT.

"Yet *another* crazy southbounder," Bawdy said.

"How'd you know the flash would scare it off, Flubby?"

"I didn't know. I just wanted a picture."

Coyote splotched with indignation, "But I coulda got sprayed."

"That," she nodded agreeably, "I did know."

"Hey," Pony wanted to know, "are we still on trail?"

Bartleby looked back the way they'd come. He couldn't see any blazes, but he felt like they must've been on trail not too long ago. They stalled at the junction of two old dirt roads and three game trails. Any and all of which could have temporarily passed for the AT. It was a nexus point of sorts and literally, the middle of nowhere. Seemed like the place used to be pastureland, but thick undergrowth was reclaiming it. There wasn't one white blaze as far as Bartleby could see, but he couldn't see too far.

"Spread out, look around," Lazy JoJo suggested. She promptly dropped her pack and settled down for a late morning snack.

Blitz, Bartleby and Pony each wandered down different paths, looking for blazes or anything else that might indicate how or where they should proceed.

In her previous life, Lazy JoJo had been a long-haul truck driver, haphazardly stitching crisscrosses back and forth from coast to coast. Wore her black hair buzzed-short and her nose smushed over to one side. She was thick-set and stocky, with a back-side that was both unnaturally and unfortunately wide and flat. Called it her "wide end" and claimed it as a consequence of thousands of hours spent behind the wheel. Was mostly deaf in her left ear, which she also blamed on long years spent rumbling over the open road. At best, her voice was rusty and rattled like a loose tailpipe. Didn't usually have much to say, but everything came out a notch or two louder than necessary.

"Y'all find anything yet? Daylight's wasting," she hollered to no one in particular.

After what couldn't have been more than a hundred yards, Bartleby's path terminated in a shallow puddle. Plenty of old hoof-prints scattered around but nothing that could've been construed as human or recent. He turned and trudged back to the clearing.

"Nothing, huh?" she asked. Before he could answer, she waved a bag at him, "Want some chocolate raisins?"

"Uh-uh."

Since Pony and Blitz still hadn't returned, Bartleby made to sit near JoJo.

"Not too close," she warned. "Got me a farty party going in my pants."

He shifted back a little ways.

"Don't talk much, do ya, Bartleby?" She smiled crookedly, "Don't get me wrong, I'm not one for lots of drama and what all. Got three sisters, call 'em Blab and Yammer and Yak. Started driving truck cuz all the gossip and gabbing made my head hurt.

"After living in a rig for twenty-three years, this doctor tells me my ticker's about tocked out. Too much durned stress, no exercise, long hours, truck-stop food and," she waved a hand all around, "I figured, one way or the other, this here trail would solve my problems."

The rising sun was shining in through new leaves. Dappled light played across the ground. Just enough breeze to cool the sweat on Bartleby's arms and legs. At least, he felt the breeze wherever the last few days of mud and grime hadn't accumulated too thickly.

"Make the NOC tomorrow, huh?"

"Guess so," Bartleby shrugged. He wondered what an NOC was.

"Definitely looking forward to a shower," JoJo was absently shifting and wiggling her wide-end down into her pack. "Got me some itching and burning ain't gonna stop without a good hot shower." She spit. "You wouldn't believe all the different ways driving can ruin a body. Hell, I'm living proof and I don't believe it. I'm about deaf in this ear from all the wind and road noise. Started clenching down on my jaw, you know, from stress. Actually cracked a molar. See? Had it yanked. My lower back's gone totally kerflooey from all the sitting. And don't even get me started about the hemorrhoids."

When Blitz and Pony returned neither had any better idea where the AT might've gone off to. "Better take a break then," Lazy JoJo advised.

"But we're lost," Pony Express said.

"Trust me, I been lost more times than all y'alls ever kissed your mamas. When ya can't find your way, sometimes it's easiest to sit back and let your way find you."

Sure enough, it wasn't a handful of minutes that passed before someone came thumping along trail. They first saw a big heroic chin, followed closely by a little guy with a ponytail.

"What is all this? Little early for lunch," Poohbah said.

"Elevenses," Pony Express garbled through a mouthful of vanilla cookies.

Poohbah looked at his watch, "Not even ten yet."

"Second breakfast then."

"We lost trail," Bartleby added.

Poohbah rolled his eyes and pointed along an unlikely looking path they hadn't investigated yet, "Goes over through there." He snorted once and left them sitting there.

"Fifteen-two, fifteen-four and a three card run for seven. What'cha got, Skunks?"

"Just a pair. And nuttin' in the crib."

"You got the right jack."

"Oh yeah."

"And you missed a fifteen in your hand, Donk."

"Where?"

"Six and nine."

"Shit. Thanks."

"You know, I'm starting to think I would really enjoy playing cribbage with the fellows who let you win two whole tournaments."

Trail etiquette is an umbrella term for the unwritten rules by which hikers are expected to conduct themselves on trail. These rules are good neighbor common sense suggestions and not so different from those already governing everyday polite society.

Hikers should endeavor to keep a small footprint in communal areas (shelters, tenting sites and hostels). This refers to sights, sounds and smells as much as it does actual square footage. Don't blind others with your headlamp like Flutterby. If people are trying to sleep, don't recite Monty Python skits in a grating British accent like Bawdy. Don't fart to clear out the shelter like Skunkers. Don't smoke at the table like Shaggy Bob. Being in the woods doesn't make second-hand smoke any less deadly or disgusting.

Be considerate. Give fellow hikers what privacy you can. Don't be a Coyote and watch from the corner of your eye whenever a woman changes clothes.

Just because you live in the woods doesn't mean you can act like an animal. Don't be lazy at night and pee close to other tenters like JoJo. Don't let your scrotum constantly flop out of your shorts like Wham-O.

Don't let your dog run loose like Nickleback. A heavily trafficked, man-made hiking trail is not the place for setting dogs free. Few dogs adjust well to trail life and fewer pay taxes, so don't assume they have the same rights as hikers. And there isn't a living soul who goes on the AT hoping to step in or otherwise encounter dog poop.

Don't shamelessly beg bites from everyone's dinner like Nickleback's dog, Lancelot.

Don't be constantly on the phone like Ella. No one wants to hear the jingling ring of your electronics, let alone endure an entire one-sided conversation.

Pack it in, pack it out and leave no trace. Don't let empty candy bar wrappers fall out of your pants pocket like Bartleby. Don't leave unburied excrement and toilet paper in your wake like Squirtz.

Don't be a volunteer trail etiquette enforcement officer, pointlessly raging over minor infringements like Poohbah.

I'm going downhill, Bawdy thought for the thousandth time. This should be easy.

From Wesser Bald it was six miles down to the Nantahala River. During those six miles, the trail lost about 3,000 feet of elevation. Worked out to 500 feet per mile. Which meant, on average, the trail declined a single measly foot for every ten feet it advanced. Graphed on paper, it would look practically level. Out on the AT, the reality looked impractically choppy. In the course of a hundred feet, the trail could drop twelve feet over the first fifteen feet, gain seven over the next thirty and drop twenty over forty only to gain another six in the last fifteen. Trending downward, sure, but not in any way that made downhill hiking easy or enjoyable. In Bawdy's limited opinion, sharp declines were far worse than sharp inclines. Sure it was tough trudging steeply uphill, but you could do it blindfolded. It was safe and steady. Just keep putting one foot in front of the other, allow for the occasional pause to let your heart stop hammering in your chest and eventually the summit would present itself. In contrast, declines didn't require so much brute force as a finite control of one's balance, foot placement and momentum. An already difficult undertaking exacerbated by the burden of an extra however many pounds of unwieldy and high-riding baggage. Misstep, lose control or just space out for a second and you could find yourself falling backward, stumbling forward or even tumbling ass-over-elbows off the trail.

Bawdy's toes were boxed tight into the front of his boots and screaming hot with friction. His quads thrummed with fine-motor fatigue. Wrists and shoulders ached from the sudden pressure of arresting his momentum or entirely catching himself and averting a spill with hiking poles. Without them, he'd have gone careening off trail a number of times already on this descent alone. It was painstaking work which, if you didn't respect the downhills with patience and composure, could quickly turn painful.

Two days earlier, they'd all spent a night in Franklin, but still, he was looking forward to a shower, a big meal and a little downtime at the Nantahala Outdoor Center. He'd not heard anything about the place, but the name alone had him optimistic. Conjured up images of a laidback woodsy retreat.

Bawdy began to think his optimism was misplaced when he was still a half mile out. He could already hear the sharp bark of loudspeakers mixed with the murmur of distant crowd noise.

"Sounds sort of different than I imagined," Flutterby called from behind.

Bawdy started, lost his balance and would've gone down but for two fortunately-placed saplings that broke his fall. "Gaaaa! You can't sneak up like that."

"Been back here for most of a mile. Couldn't figure why you weren't letting me pass."

"Sorry," he said. "Didn't hear you. Thought I was alone."

"*I'm* sorry—look at you," she said while taking a hold of his pack and yanking him upright, out of the entangling branches.

The last bit of trail looped down, smoothed out and deposited them along the southern bank of the Nantahala River. There were cars and colors and crap everywhere. Far as he could tell, the milling crowds were mostly spectators, watching whitewater kayakers as they raced down the rapids. Bawdy'd lived in Chicago for the last four years, so of course he wasn't a stranger to bustling crowds and street noise, but the short time he'd spent in the woods had apparently skewed his expectations downward. What would have seemed perfectly normal a month ago, now seemed so over-stimulating and awful he could only gape at the sheer spectacle of it.

There was a certain in-your-face terribleness to it all, exacerbated by Bawdy's sudden comprehension that this scene, more than any other, best represented the *real* America.

Booming loudspeakers, the cheer of beer-drinking tourists (these mostly stuffed tight into bathing trunks and ill-fitting bikinis), honking horns, neon banners and flashing billboards.

"This is something, huh?" Flutterby said before starting off to cross the street.

"It's Gomorrah all over again," Bawdy mumbled, following her lead. He had to dodge oncoming traffic and got honked at for the effort.

They sat on an empty bench. Dazedly processing their surroundings for a few minutes. Wasn't too long before Coyote and Skunkers came rolling off trail.

"Wow," Coyote said, "are we staying here?" He already had his data book out, was figuring options. "The climb out of here is a full seven miles. No camping, no water, nothing but *up* until Sassafras Gap. I really don't want to hike anymore, but...."

"I'm staying," Flutterby said. "I've got a maildrop waiting for me."

What followed was the inevitable domino effect. Coyote stayed because Flutterby was staying (he pretty much followed her like an imprinted duckling). Skunkers stayed because Coyote was staying (seemed like a good time to collect on the beers Coyote owed him). Bawdy stayed because Flutterby, Coyote and Skunkers were all staying (he had no desire to go off alone and risk losing them like he'd somehow lost Bartleby, plus he seriously doubted he could survive a seven mile climb that afternoon).

"I'll go see what they've got for rooms," Flutterby said.

She returned ten minutes later with four Coors Light tall

boys. Handed them around. "We got options. A four man bunkroom costs eighty dollars. Course, I know we only got like a man and a half between us, but the rate doesn't change. I asked."

"*Or?*"

"Or this dude offered to let me sleep in his barn. Says it's just a coupla miles down the road."

"What dude?"

"Over there—wearing the faded black t-shirt."

"Just you or all of us?"

"Dunno. All of us, I guess."

"That's one shifty mo-fo," Coyote said. "And I think I would know a little something about shifty mo-fos." He turned and said "Count that," to Bawdy before continuing. "Barn-boy looks like a pervert. A murderer at the very least."

"He might be okay," she said. "Would save us each twenty bucks."

"You're crazy, Flubby. Listen—I'll pay your share, you big beautiful beer-buying dope. Don't get yourself locked in some sex dungeon-cum-hayloft just to save twenty dollars. It would just shrivel my heart up."

Skunkers popped the tab on his beer, raised it to his lips and sucked. Drank so fast, the sides of the can dimpled with each glug. Downed the whole thing, gently burped into his fist, "When I got back, I made a promise to myself. We stay in that guy's barn, there's at least a fifty percent chance he's gonna make me break that promise."

"You promise to give up your secret love of livestock?"

"No, smartass. I promised to stop killing people."

After taking care of the standard chores, they sequestered themselves in the bunkroom. Theoretically away from all the obnoxious noise.

"Higher. Hold the light higher," Ella said. Somehow she had spotted them, pushed her way into the room and roped Coyote into playing camera man for one of her video blogs. Skunkers was sprawled back on a top bunk, fiddling with his computer watch. Every so often he shared a pronouncement, the current elevation or barometric reading. Gospel as told to him by his wrist-watch.

"Down to seventy-one degrees. Barometer holding steady at 31.20."

"You need to stop shaking the camera. I can see it shaking."

Flutterby and Bawdy had started a game of Scrabble. On her second turn, Flutterby had bingoed (F-A-S-T-I-N-G on an open E for FEASTING) and Bawdy was painstakingly trying to comeback with a bingo of his own.

"Put down a word already, Bawds."

"How's about a little patience? It's only been my turn for a few minutes."

Flutterby raised an eyebrow, "Skunkers?"

"Nine minutes, thirty-six seconds. Thirty-seven, thirty-eight, thir—"

Bawdy fumbled four tiles on the board.

To Skunkers, Flutterby said, "Thanks." To Bawdy she said, "GIFTS? You couldn't find a better use for the S than that?"

"Hey—hike your own hike, will ya?"

"Ready, Yote? Okay, roll it. Hi, this is Ella Smith coming to you from a bunkroom at the Nantahala Outdoor Center, or NOC, here in Wesser, North Carolina. It's currently six twenty-one—"

"I got six twenty-four," Skunkers corrected.

"—and seventy-one degrees. Today's hike was all about gravity. Some eleven miles back, the trail peaked at Copper Ridge Bald Lookout. A high of five thousand eighty feet. Since then, it's been a doozy of a downhill drop to seventeen hundred twenty-three feet at the banks of the rushing Nantahala River."

"I got seventeen seventy-eight up here, so you're probably something like seventeen seventy-four and a half."

Ella looked over, wasted a hard-eye glare on the oblivious Skunkers before turning back to find Coyote had taken the opportunity to slow pan the camera down the length of her body. "Keep the camera up here, Yote. On my face."

"Thought you wanted these to be interesting?"

"If I had one get-out-of-jail-free card," Bawdy grumbled, "I honestly don't know which one of you I'd strangle."

Flutterby giggled, "Would've been more peaceful at that guy's barn, even if he was a psycho sex predator."

When Ella finished filming, she took a seat next to Bawdy, "I wanna play."

"And I wanna be a famous novelist, but we're in the middle of a ga—"

He didn't even finish the sentence before Ella jostled the board, sent the tiles skittering out of place.

"Oops," she said. "That was totally clumsy of me."

❦

Skunkers and Coyote were up in the two top bunks, drinking beers and spiraling an empty water bottle back and forth like it was a football.

Bawdy waited for Ella to take her turn. She was a slower player than he was, and that was saying something. Worse still, she felt it necessary to thoroughly explain her decision making process.

"See, I can't go there or I'll open up the triple for Flutterby. And if I had a D, I could put it here, make DAFT and DARK. Score something like twenty-nine points. Or if I had a X, I could put it there after your ZA. Spell OXEN and ZAX, which is a tool for cutting—"

"Roof tiles," Bawdy blurted. "I know what a zax is, Ella. Please stop talking and make a word. Any word."

Skunkers monkeyed down from the bunk, stepped just outside the bunkroom door, and proceeded to audibly urinate. From her seat, Flutterby could see him swaying unsteadily in the darkness.

"That makes me so mad," she mumbled.

Ella, who had been reaching to place tiles, stopped short, "I know, right? Disgusting. We don't want to see that, Skunkers."

"I don't care about seeing it. I'm jealous. Guys can just pee anywhere and it's such a production for us. I had to troop a hundred yards over to the shower room to do the same damn thing."

Ella placed the tiles back on her rack, began reconsidering her options.

Bawdy blew out a snort of annoyance, set to cleaning his glasses. Seemed like the lenses were perpetually smudged over with sweat-streaks.

Coyote called down, "What's the matter with your spoon, Bawds?"

He'd been using it to stir his soup and left it standing in the pot with the water boiling. The spoon handle had wilted, drooped down over the pot edge. Looked like something Salvador Dali might've used to eat his morning cereal. Stupid thing was supposed to be impervious to heat.

"Fuckfuckfuckfuck." Bawdy plucked the melted spoon out of the soup and burned his fingers in the process.

Coyote was wheezing with laughter, sounded more than a little like a hyena with pneumonia.

"Never fear, Bawds," Skunkers tossed him a titanium spork, "I got your back."

"Thanks, man. I'll clean it and get it back to you pronto."

"You can keep it. It's my just-in-case backup."

"A just-in-case backup spoon?" Coyote's cheeks glistened with tears. "You two could be an Aesop Fable. The idgit and the ox. The one's too stupid to boil water, the other thinks he can carry the whole world on his back."

Register: Sassafras Gap Shelter

4/17 North Carolina
    boggy gaps, grassy balds, bloom-
    ing rhododendron

                    High-Ku

✤ ✤ ✤

Cheoah Bald. It wasn't so much a true grassy dome-topped mountain, as a grassy south-facing slope. Still and all, a nice place to sit, enjoy the view and eat Slim Jims by the handful in the afternoon sun.

Which is exactly what Pony Express was doing when Bartleby showed up.

"Nice view, huh?"

"Unh."

"Some climb up, huh?

"Unh."

"Want a Slim Jim?"

"Unh."

✤ ✤ ✤

As the edges of night slowly fizzled away, Flutterby lay cocooned and comfy in her hammock. The boys had pitched their tents near the intersection of the AT and a blue-blazed trail. She'd set up a little ways off amongst some high scrub. Because of the hammock's arboreal nature, she could set up on sloped or overgrown terrain and other areas that no sane tenter would have reasonably considered.

As much as giving herself privacy, she did this to give the boys some privacy from her. As the only woman among three men, she didn't want to smother them with her presence, overly curb male instincts or infringe on fraternal bonding. Bawdy, Coyote and Skunkers couldn't have been more different from each other or from Flutterby's expectations of the opposite sex. For all that, she liked and felt comfortable around them, both individually and as a pack. This appreciation made her very conscious of not wanting to overstay her welcome. It was surprising to see how quickly and easily the shared experience of thru-hiking forged relationships among people who might not have had a single common interest if they'd met off trail.

Flutterby was awake, had been since before first light. She lay there, dreamily content, listening to the birds and looking out at the natural world.

Distanced as she was from all the snoring and rustling of synthetic fabrics, she couldn't help but wake with the first stirring cheep. From there, it slowly built into an erratic but pleasing medley of chiding chirps, warbled wooing, cheeping peeps and tweeting twitters.

They weren't anything fancy. They were the barn swallows, wrens, wood thrushes and dark-eyed juncos; the ordinary and commonplace of the avian masses; often overlooked and sometimes underfoot. Flutterby didn't mind the bird's commonplace roots, it had quickly become her favorite time of day.

As she listened, the birdcalls went uncharacteristically quiet. Some ways off, maybe seventy yards, Flutterby noticed movement. A man's form appeared from amongst the underbrush. He was followed closely by the low shape of a hound and a dozen paces back, a second man. Hunters. The first carried a long gun in the crook of his arm, the other's was slung over his shoulder. They wore equal parts realistic looking camouflage and reflective orange. Their progress over the forest floor was so smooth and quiet, she wondered if they followed a game trail. It was unlikely she would've even noticed them if she hadn't been alerted by the sudden absence of bird song.

From inside her hammock, she watched the men approach the tents. They never slowed; simply stepped around backpacks and over guy lines. The hound sniffed once at Bawdy's tarp before loping to catch up.

The hunters and their hound melted away, back into the forest, out of sight and gone before Flutterby realized she was holding her breath.

❧ ❧ ❧

"Fug."
"Fugley."
"Frig."
"Frigging."
"Fig."

❧ ❧ ❧

It was almost eight-thirty at night when Two-Speed Tortoise finally limped down the paved side trail to the Fontana Dam Shelter.

Her feet burned. Her knees throbbed. Her thighs felt like old jelly. White salt soaked through her clothes. Every part of her body that could rub against something else, had been doing exactly that for the last four hours. Upper arms, inner thighs, nipples under her faded red sports bra, even the cheeks of her ass were chafed and stinging.

Eyes sunken, throat dry, lips cracked. Brain frazzled and

fried. She wanted to cry, had done so seven miles back. Couldn't now; not enough liquids left. Too tired and dried out for tears.

The shelter was big and civilized. Had access to running water and real bathrooms. The guidebooks called it the Fontana Dam Hilton. In a pinch, it could accommodate forty hikers. Probably about half that were milling around when she arrived.

Hairbrained was sitting there on a bench, drinking a soda, looking out at the reservoir and bullshitting with other hikers.

"Oh, hey, babe," he looked at his watch, grimaced. "Jesus, you took your time, didn't you? I figured you'd be in before eight, easy." He called over, raised his watch up, "Hey, Shaggy Bob—guess I owe you a beer."

She'd been trying to think what to say to him for the last eleven-point-six miles. Hadn't come up with much that could be shared in polite company. The plan had been simple. Hike sixteen miles from the NOC to Brown Fork Gap Shelter. Wake up the next morning and cruise the eleven-point-six into Fontana Dam by noon. The first seven miles out of the NOC were relentlessly uphill. The trail didn't even pretend to do anything but climb towards the sky. She'd kept up with him for the first few miles, but then she started to flag, and he pulled away. Arrived at Brown Fork Gap only to learn that he'd gone ahead, continued on to Fontana Dam without waiting for her, without talking it over, without sticking to the plan they'd laid out.

"Why," she said, her voice sounding like crushed gravel, "did I hike twenty-seven-point-six miles today?"

He finished off the last of the soda, "What'd'ya mean?"

"Why aren't we back at Brown Gap Shelter, like we planned?"

"Brown *Fork* Gap Shelter," he corrected. "You forgot the Fork."

"Maybe I was saving the *fork* to jab in your eye." She was talking slowly, and trembling now with rage and fatigue and hunger.

"What's you problem? I left a note in the register."

"I saw the note. 'Tortoise: You are too slow. Been waiting for days. Getting antsy. Going ahead to the Hilton. See you there.'"

"I figured you would stay back at Brown Fork Gap. Figured I'd save time. Could go in, resupply and meet you back here by lunchtime. Figured—"

"How was I going to stay back there without *you*?"

"You've got your own food and the tent."

"And you're carrying our stove and water filter. Did you figure that?"

Hairbrained opened his mouth, but for a blessed little while nothing came out of it.

"You're gonna be right behind, Skunks?"

"Just gotta skip down to the post office, get my food squared away. Take me an hour, two max," he assured them. "The way you three hike, I'll probably still beat y'all up to Mollies Ridge."

"A pint of Ben & Jerry's says I beat you to Mollies Ridge by three hours."

"You can book that bet, Slick."

Bawdy, Coyote and Flutterby left Skunkers at the Fontana Hilton, made their way over Fontana Dam. A wide, paved roadway went across the top. The metallic tips of their hiking poles ticked and tacked against the pavement. The trio, freshly showered and resupplied, were warmed by the late morning sun. A wide blue reservoir to their right, a four hundred eighty foot drop on their left. They stopped to peer down the full length of the dam's face. The extreme height and sheer angle of the dam was generally terrifying.

After a couple hundred yards the AT swooped off the pavement and scrambled its way up into the Great Smoky Mountains of Tennessee.

❦

Skunkers got off to a later start than planned. Took almost an hour to hitch down to the village. Turned out the trip was only three miles, he could've walked it in less time than he spent waiting for a ride. Once there, it took a while to sort out his maildrop and bolster those supplies with selections from the general store. The hitch back was quicker. he got started hiking two hours later than he'd hoped, a full hour later than he'd honestly expected. Hustled over the dam, didn't waste time sight-seeing, taking pictures or perusing the little visitor center. Found a hiking trail and bounded upwards along it. Still hoping to win himself some ice cream.

Took most of an hour for him to realize and finally admit that he wasn't on the AT. Wasn't sure if he ever had been. Couldn't exactly recall seeing a single blaze all day. Far as he knew, he could've been on the wrong trail right from the get go.

Luckily, Skunkers carried a fistful of topographic maps. He sorted through until he found one that showed all of Smoky Mountain National Park. That slick-mouthed Coyote kept busting his hump for packing along so much seemingly useless shit, but who was laughing now? Skunkers carried the maps because he liked to see where he was and where he was going in relation to the wider world. Liked to know what else was out there beyond the immediate range of his sight. It took little time to place himself on the map. Wasn't so bad. Looked like he could go back about four miles to where he'd accidentally branched left off the AT or he could keep on for a bit, catch a squiggly little trail somewhere ahead on his right and rejoin the AT in six or eight miles. This second course, being the hypotenuse of the triangle, looked to be significantly shorter than backtracking.

So Skunkers continued along in the wrong direction. After a quarter hour, he couldn't help wondering if he'd somehow missed the little trail that was supposed to squiggle off to the right. There hadn't been posted signs or obvious forks in the road, nothing but scrub growth and high, leafy trees. He plowed ahead for another few minutes before giving up. Studied the map some more and made a command decision. Instead of continuing to look for this hidden trail that, if it actually existed, he'd already missed once, Skunkers decided to cut easterly and bushwhack overland. Essentially make make his own squiggly trail reconnecting with the AT.

All went well with this new plan, until he came upon a fast flowing stream that had looked much smaller on the map. Flush with spring runoff, it was too deep for him to cross without thoroughly soaking his boots and risking a dunk. He followed it a ways, looking for a place to cross without getting wet. Best he found was a wide, gravelly spot. Seemed a bit shallower, but not much. He removed boots, stuffed his wool socks down into them and knotted laces together. Slipped on flip-flops, hung the boots over his shoulder and took a few preparatory breaths on the bank.

The tumbling water looked cold and felt colder.

Both feet wet, then his shins and knees. At its highest the water reached to mid-thigh. Skunkers' breath came in shallow gasps; his heart felt like it might be coming up and out his throat. It wasn't all sandy gravel beneath him either, lots of round river rocks too, and these were as slick and slippery as Coyote. All told, Skunkers had to cross fifteen feet of running water. Lost his footing in the last five, stumbled, almost went down. Would have without his hiking poles. He got his feet back under himself in time to watch one of his flip-flops float away. When he stepped onto the far bank he had one bare foot and a mouthful of chattering teeth.

Once re-booted, Skunkers continued crunching through underbrush. He noticed curious flimmering clouds exploding out from each footfall. When he stooped low, he saw thousands of tiny brown grasshoppers, newly hatched and nearly invisible against the forest floor. That is, until they scattered before his advance with a rustling that sounded like a popping bowl of Rice Krispies.

So it was over the river and through the woods to Mollies Ridge Shelter he went. Skunkers found two more streams to ford (for all he knew they could've all been the same damn one) before finally stumbling across the AT. He almost missed the stupid thing as darkness settled over the land. It turned out he still had another five miles of rising trail to cover before setting eyes on the shelter. No moonlight to speak of, it was full dark and windy when his hiking day finally came to a close.

Skunkers snuck a peak into the shelter. It was big enough to comfortably sleep fourteen. Had a covered cooking area to one side, an old stone chimney fireplace and a big blue tarp strung across the open face to help keep the worst of the weather out. Snapped like the U.S. flag in a sand storm.

It was past eleven and he didn't want to wake anyone, especially Coyote, so he slunk off a little ways from the shelter and set up his tent. Scuffed around in his remaining flip-flop and an unlaced boot looking for the trail down to the water source. Would've used the privy if he could've found it. But since he couldn't, he cooked, ate, and climbed into his sleeping bag by midnight.

❦

"That you, Skunky?" Coyote wanted to know. "Where ya been? And more importantly—why you sleeping in a smoking shit field?"

Skunkers had been dead asleep. Took him a moment to stick his head out the tent flap, "What'r'you going on about?"

It was particularly difficult to take the little guy seriously. In addition to that stupid leer permanently stretched across his face, Coyote had some funky bed head going and he was wearing a red union suit. Stupid thing even had a back-flap, just like in old westerns.

Coyote marched past with a roll of toilet paper in hand.

In the early light, Skunkers could see the ground around him was sprinkled suspiciously with sodden white clumps. Sort of looked like wild grown bunches of cauliflower.

"The bad news," Coyote explained, "is that most of the shelters in the Smokies don't have privies. Apparently, we're all supposed to go off and dig personal catholes in which to bury our *business*. Turns out, most people don't bother so much with that. Which leaves us with a regional phenomenon I'm calling 'the smoking shit fields of Tennessee'.

"And the good news, Skunks? Well, you slept smack in the middle of one."

From where they were up on the ridgeline, the valleys to either side were completely submerged under rolling tides of smoke-colored clouds. Bawdy could see shades ranging from dark purple to shadowy blue to the white of old snow. They were walking up above the cloud banks. It felt surreal, like nothing else existed, just the trail before them and the land directly under their feet.

Somewhere after Devil's Tater Patch, Bawdy started whistling. Couldn't help himself. Pretty soon that toothy little whistle morphed into a hum. Skunkers recognized it and joined right in. Coyote would've yelled and made Bawdy shut the hell up, but not Skunkers. He went right along, he was good people. And with that tractor-beam memory of Bawdy's, it wasn't any bit of a surprise when the lyrics started tumbling around his mind like wet laundry stuffed into a dryer.

Nothing else for it but to keep on hiking and humming the

song. Over and over until they got to about where the book said it was. A stony outcrop half a mile south of Thunderhead's east peak. Bawdy went and stood up on a rock pedestal and Skunkers followed his lead. When they finished humming the song through, they started once more from the beginning. This time singing aloud the words from "Rocky Top", that old bluegrass anthem to the Tennessee hills.

They were off-key, off-tempo and out of tune. But somehow the song sounded just about perfect ringing off the ridgeline.

❦ ❦ ❦

The Smoky Mountains sucked.

And it wasn't just because of the sharp lack of privies. Plenty of other reasons why Poohbah didn't like the Smokies. Like how the AT mostly followed the ridgeline, sometimes no more than ten feet wide, and stayed up high among the peaks and crags. Made for some spectacular views, but lousy water access. Wasn't so much that the springs went dry as there just weren't many situated up so high. Or because, as a national park, the Smokies had restrictive rules for hikers. These were enforced by full-on, firearm carrying rangers and part-time, spot-check loving Ridgerunners. No dogs allowed. Had to figure out your itinerary, get a hiking permit and carry it around with you. Being a protected animal refuge, the park was chock-full of socialized black bears and antisocial boars. Both for safety reasons and to minimize environmental impact, hikers were supposed to sleep only at the designated shelter areas.

Back in '97, this wasn't such a terribly big deal. A bit

restrictive sure, but the AT wasn't really crowded then. Course, that was before Bill Bryson came out with *A Walk in the Woods* and made the AT a premier destination for every inconsiderate slob and hopeful dreamer on the planet.

Poohbah had never met the man, never laid eyes on him, never read that damn book of his, but he couldn't help but think of Bryson as "That Lazy Bastard Who Ruined Everything." With increased public awareness came the inevitable swelling in the ranks of thru-hikers coming out for the annual pilgrimage. Lots more people on trail in '01, tons more in '04 and this year looked to be the worst yet—well beyond what the trail infrastructure had ever been intended to support. Wandering individuals had been supplanted by migrating herds. Some nights Poohbah counted twenty tents circled around a packed shelter. In the morning there'd be fifteen people waiting to use the single privy. And that only where the privies hadn't been filled to spilling over, or removed entirely as was the case in the Smokies.

All of which, Poohbah put squarely on Bryson's shoulders. The guy waltzed onto trail, didn't come close to completing an actual thru-hike and still somehow managed to pied-piper a couple bajillion dummies into the woods. Poohbah seriously doubted it would ever happen, but he'd prepared and rehearsed some words just in case he ever crossed paths with That Lazy Bastard Who Ruined Everything.

❧

From his spot at the picnic table of Derrick's Knob Shelter, Poohbah could make out maybe a dozen clumps of used toilet paper left in plain sight. If he took a short stroll around the area, he knew he'd find a hundred more. It made him spitting mad.

Before he got himself all worked up thinking about it, he polished off his pre-dinner snack (half a tray of Nutter-Butter cookies), chugged the last of his water and wandered down to the spring.

About two hundred steps down and around a bend there was a little pool, no bigger than a bathroom sink. Seemed even smaller with one of Blitz' big feet cooling in it. He was sitting there like a child playing at the shore, digging out handfuls of rock and mud, excavating and expanding the pool so it could eventually accommodate both of his feet.

This was exactly the type of ignorant, inconsiderate bullshit that made Poohbah's blood boil.

"What," Poohbah said, his face purpling over, "the *fuck* are you doing?"

❧

Tension smothered the shelter that night. After initially raging at Blitz for fouling the water source, Poohbah continued to indiscriminately pepper the area with snarky comments and bad attitude. When he wasn't sniping pot-shots specifically at the German kid, he was ranting about trail etiquette and raving against the invading hordes of inconsiderate dolts.

While the language barrier certainly helped buffer Blitz from the specifics of this barrage, no way did it keep out the spite and generalized ill-will coming from Poohbah.

Lazy JoJo was stuck sitting there between them at the table, cooking dinner, minding her own business and sucking at a splintery toothpick. Pony was giving Bartleby prompting looks like maybe he should say or do something to intervene. Bartleby was either ignoring these or entirely oblivious to them; it was too close to call.

Poohbah was still going, building up a head of steam, when JoJo took that toothpick out.

"Alright there, Captain Appalachia," she said. Her voice a steady scrape of old metal. "That's about all I can take on an empty stomach."

Poohbah stopped mid-sentence, his mouth hanging wide.

"The kid apologized. I'm betting he won't do it again. Give it a rest."

"You can't tell me—"

"I can tell you I'd rather drink dirty foot water than listen to all your assholery."

"If—"

She leaned in close. A gargoyle grimace revealed a crooked set of nicotine stained teeth, "*If* ya keep talking, I'm *gonna* make ya cry."

Register: Double Spring Gap Shelter

4/22 Has anyone noticed how quickly hikers come up and reel off their resume? Earlier in the week this couple didn't say hi, didn't smile, just started right in on how they were celebrating the 5th anniversary of their thru-hike. Good for you I guess but, why do I care exactly? So I started counting. When you meet a new hiker it usually doesn't take more than a few sentences for them to spit their hiking resume at you. The coolest hang back for a whole 2 minutes. Flippin' crazy how everyone's so damn frantic to establish trail cred. Seems like all Peace Corps Volunteers I've met do this too. They can't wait to tell you about how many squash they planted in Uganda or whatever. As if that somehow defines them. I'm dubbing this phenomenon the PCV Effect in their honor and writing it up for the Journal of Popular Psychology.

-Dr. Bawdy Boy, MS, MA, MFA, Ph.D.

4/22 Way back on Springer, when I first met you, you told me all about your degrees before you ever told me your name. Just one of the many reasons I went to bed so early that first night.

Nurse Flubby Bubby, R.N.

When she finally reached the top of Clingmans Dome, Flutterby was more than a little disappointed. Firstly, it wasn't nearly as dramatically mountainous a summit as she'd been expecting. Instead of rocky peaks or windswept cliffs, an alpine forest completely covered the dome.

Secondly, with an auto-road leading up to it and the ugly, concrete observation curlicue built on top, the spot was unfortunately "civilized." At 6,643 feet above sea level, it was the highest point along the entire AT. Instead of feeling remotely romantic though, it felt touristy and paved over. Lots of sight-seers were milling around, most had motored to within a few hundred yards of the summit and waddled the last little bit. She wouldn't ever admit it aloud, but she found it off-putting to see so many fat people again. Back at the hospital, working with seriously obese patients had always freaked her out. Flut-terby didn't realize it until that moment, but there was an obvious lack of really fat people on trail. One way or the other, she guessed, they didn't survive too long out in the woods. They either got thin or they got off trail right quick.

From up on the observation tower, the 360-degree view was fine. More expansive than straight up majestic. She had her camera in hand, had been planning to get a bunch of photos.

"Want me to take your picture," Bawdy offered.

"Thanks, but I'm thinking I don't want to remember this place."

"Well, I do," Coyote said, "here take one of me and Flubby Pie." He tossed his camera to Bawdy and quick draped a famil-iar arm around Flutterby's shoulders.

"How do I zoom in?" Bawdy took so long fiddling with the buttons, Flutterby had shrugged Coyote off and stepped away by the time he got things figured out.

"Okay. Smile, Yote."

"Forget it—was a beautiful moment and you missed it, Molasses."

When they wandered down from the observation tower, they found Skunkers on a bench, working a corkscrew into a big bottle of wine.

"Where'd ya get that?" Bawdy asked.

"Back at Fontana. Figured we could celebrate reaching the

top of the world here.

"You carried a magnum of cheap wine all the way from Fontana Village? It's like thirty miles and that bottle's gotta weigh at least five, six pounds." Coyote was visibly appalled, "What's the matter with you?"

When the cork plocked free, Skunkers just sniffed it and grinned.

❧

It was getting on towards the dark side of dusk by the time they polished off the wine and roped a tourist into recycling the bottle back in civilization for them. Still another three miles to the next shelter. The hiking was mostly downhill, which, considering they'd just caught a buzz up on the tippy top of the AT, made perfect sense. Wasn't strenuous but the footing was tricky and, even with his headlamp shining down bright, the shifting shadows played hell on Bawdy's eyes and his wine-wet mind.

Apparently it wasn't a problem the others shared as they quickly outpaced him. Skunkers was leading them in an amusingly raunchy marching song, something about meeting the farmer's daughter. But even that faded away until only occasional faint snatches came wafting back down the trail.

There was a mile left to go when Bawdy heard a grunting noise behind him. It was loud enough that he felt he should turn to investigate, but also loud enough to make that seem like a very bad idea. He stood there trying to think which course of action might play out worse for him. When he finally did turn around, the white light of his headlamp reflected back from two close set eyes about eighteen inches off the ground. He couldn't discern even a vague outline of the body that went along with those eyes. Some nocturnal animal, most likely a young black bear or a wild sow on an evening wander, out to see what was what in the world.

There was a doglike snuffling that might've come from Bawdy or from whatever owned those two eyes staring back at him. He'd never know for sure. With a sharp snort the eyes were gone.

❧

Sometime in that last mile of his night hike, Bawdy decided to treat himself to Peace Pasta Parm. It had already been a standout day and he thought to cap it off properly and pamper himself when he got to the shelter.

Annie's Homegrown Organic Peace Pasta with Parmesan was a designer mac and cheese. It was seemingly created to appease those cursed with both a discerning palate and the pocket-lint finances of an academic. In Bawdy's epicurean opinion, P3 was the very apex, acme and zenith of all cheesy pasta meals served straight out of a box. And after ten years living on ridiculously small stipends and otherwise skimping on the finer things, he should know. The pastas were fashioned in the shape of circular peace signs and came complete with a reconstituted garlic-parm-cheddar cheese powder that was second to none. At something like three times the price of a Kraft mac and cheese, P3 was a special luxury, a rare treat. It had arrived in Bawdy's last maildrop and he'd put off eating it the last few nights, simply enjoying the fact that the meal was looming on his horizon and jostling in his food bag. The mere knowledge that he could eat it anytime acted as a sort of carrot, leading him on through the long hiking days.

With the decision locked in, his anticipation and appetite escalated exponentially with every step.

At the shelter, Bawdy immediately set to cooking up his feast. He couldn't even wait to go and get his own water, borrowing some instead from Flutterby. With the others already cooking dinner, the shelter table was littered with water bottles, cook stoves and food bags.

Bawdy shouldered his way onto the bench seat, "Scoot over, Skunkers. I got me a feast to whip up."

"Seriously, dude? I'm already half in Flubby's lap."

"It's okay," she said, "I can move down a little more."

"Go sit next to Yote," Skunkers growled. He was a lefty and liked to have plenty of room for his spork arm. Dinner was the most serious event in the daily routine of thru-hikers. And a trencherman like Skunkers, well, he took it more seriously than most.

"Scoot it or I'm gonna boot it, ya big bumpkin," Bawdy joked. "Peace Pasta Parm waits for no man."

Squirtz shifted his pot lid and food sack out of the way.

"Thanks, Squirtz. See? There's plenty of room here for everyone, Skunky."

When his water started to boil, Bawdy added the peace-shaped pastas. Kept the pot over the flame, checked it often, stirred it lovingly and, literally, smacked his lips.

"You sound like a dog I used to have."

"Too hungry to care, Flubby Pie."

"Did your dog have dorko glasses and a mullet?" Coyote asked.

"This ain't no mullet. Blue-collar rednecks have mullets. Poet-philosophers such as myself have romantically shaggy locks."

"I'm a blue-collar redneck," Skunkers said.

"So?"

"So. I don't got no mullet or shaggy locks or nothing else."

"And that," Bawdy countered merrily, "is the exception that proves the rule."

"Yeah? What's that mean?"

"Absolutely nothing. Mostly it's an idiom used by idiots, but I can't tell you how many students I've shut up and shot down with it."

Coyote snorted, "Bet you were one of those jackass teachers I woulda hated. I'm allergic to stuffed shirts."

Memories of time spent leading a classroom brought a grin to Bawdy's face, "Dude, I was the world's windiest d-bag. Pretentious and portentous both. I was like a corrupt magistrate ruling over some poor little village way out on the fringes of the empire. Lording over the ignorant peasants with the clenched fist of hypocrisy and the open-handed karate chop of indiscriminate bias.

"Students would come argue their grades during my office hours. It was a point of pride with me to make sure nine out of ten left with lower grades. I'd comb through their essays line-by-line and point out all the mistakes. I cannot even honestly guesstimate how many freshmen I've made cry. And not just the girls—you'd be surprised. I was," Bawdy summed up, "an inflectiously sarcastic, ball-busting hard-on of such throbbingly officious proportions, that I often despised myself." He shrugged, "It was awesome."

"Sounds way worse than Basic training," Skunkers said.

His pasta now cooked, Bawdy stirred in the powdered cheese, covered it up and set it aside to thicken into a work of culinary high art.

He must've still been feeling the wine, because he started up talking again, unprompted, "Yeah, I was bad. Don't know why exactly, or when it started, but I had this little tradition of humming *The Imperial March* to myself as I went down to teach class. Like I was a Sith Lord heading off to crush rebel scum."

"And what's that?" Flutterby asked.

"Oh, you know, that Darth Vader song. Goes like," Bawdy rapped out the beat with his knuckles as he boomed along, "Bum, bum, bum, ba ba-bum—"

He was a bit overzealous though and sloppy-fisted. Accidentally brought his hand cracking down on the handle of his cook pot. Sent the Peace Pasta Parm catapulting through the air.

Some of the scalding hot peace-shaped pastas landed on the table top and the bench seat. More landed on Bawdy's stomach, his lap and his bare legs. The vast majority landed on the dirt at his feet.

The shocked silence that enveloped the shelter area was finally broken by the wheezing riot of Coyote's laughter.

"Uh-oh," Skunkers said, taking his cue from Coyote, "Spaghetti-O's."

Far as Bartleby could tell, Newfound Gap was nothing more than a huge parking lot full of cars and the touristy-types who drove them. He would've bypassed it entirely, but the trail cut across the auto-road and the parking lot before dodging back into the woods.

It was early afternoon and he'd not quite made it across the parking lot when an older couple corralled him. "Are you thru-hiking, young man?"

He nodded.

"What's your name?" the woman wanted to know.

"Bartleby."

"Ooooh—like the wine coolers?"

"What's your ruck weigh, son?"

"Dunno. Fifty pounds, maybe."

"That's good." The man nodded knowingly.

"Oh, that sounds heavy. Is it heavy? It looks heavy," she said.

"It's pretty heavy," Bartleby admitted.

"It's *too* heavy," she suggested.

"It's not *too* heavy, Milly. He's come all the way from Springer. You came from Springer, didn't you son?"

Bartleby nodded.

"How many miles is that?"

"Dunno. Long way."

"See, Milly. He's already come a fair piece," the man gestured across the parking lot. "We came on down from Iowa. Got us one of those live-aboard RV's. Come spring, we get out and visit a new section of country. Come on over. We'll give you an iced tea and a tour of the rig."

Register: Icewater Spring Shelter

4/23   A woman give me flat, lukewarm soda and stale
       graham crackers back at the Gap. For the sake of
       journalistic accuracy in my blog, is she a trail angel
       or simply cleaning out cupboards?   Ella

"Wish someone would give me lukewarm soda and stale graham crackers," Coyote whined. "That goddamned girl keeps running into all sorts of trail magic and trail angels and whatever else is out here. Now she's all but complaining about it, and here I am, can't get a helping hand or a free calorie to save my life."

"You could shadow her," Bawdy suggested.

"What's that?"

"You know, spend a day or two hiking behind her. Literally. Hang back a couple hundred yards or so. Then you'll be in position to get in on any trail magic she stumbles across."

Coyote thought this over, finally shook his head, "Don't need handouts *that* bad."

For Pony Express, the high mountain meadows were easily the best part of the Smokies. The occasional level patches of open ground were thinly carpeted with ankle-high flowers. Instead of boasting a robust diversity, these meadows radiated a fragile elegance, a lonely simplicity that he could relate to. Threadbare blankets of pink-veined Spring Beauties or propeller-shaped Bluets spread over rocky soil.

Because the AT traversed an elevated ridge-line for most of its time in the park, interesting bird sightings were minimal. Pony considered himself lucky to have spotted a Northern Saw-whet Owl. Of course the little guy didn't do anything but huddle and perch, half-hidden up high behind the incoming foliage. As owls went, the Northern Saw-whet was relatively commonplace, so Pony didn't spend hours staking it out, waiting to hear its call. Conversely, he heard but didn't see an Olive-sided Flycatcher. This was a good trade-off, as they were olive-gray-brown in color, smallish and non-descript looking.

The worst part of the Smokies was the privy down at Peck's Corner Shelter. The shelter was so far off trail (point-five), Pony would never have gone down to it, but for the rumor that it possessed an actual working privy. Far as he knew, it was one of only a spare few to be found throughout the entire park.

Sure, there might've been some weird science to it, some engineering imperatives or ecological necessities limiting the places where the privy could be located. Just as likely that the installation crew had a wicked sense of humor. Logical or comical motives notwithstanding, they'd situated the privy between the AT and the shelter, no more than two feet off the shelter trail. Bad enough, you couldn't arrive at or leave the shelter without walking within sniffing distance, but then they went ahead and built the privacy screen only waist high. Even the shortest hikers would be wholly exposed if they did anything but sit down before dropping trou.

Come morning, Pony experienced the expected urge to use the facility. This was the reason he'd elected to stay over at Peck's Corner. But when he marched up to the privy, he balked at the line. Half a dozen hikers queued up not ten feet from the privy structure, which was currently and quite obviously occupied by JoJo. He could see her rolling that toothpick side-to-side in her mouth. No way could Pony comfortably apply himself under that sort of open air scrutiny. He went back down to the shelter, fidgeted with his gear and shifted from foot to foot until he figured the crowd had thinned out.

Luckily it had. He got himself settled down and promptly focused on the task at hand without an audience.

It wasn't too long before Blitz lumbered past on his way back up to the AT. Pony hadn't the slightest idea what might constitute an appropriate interaction at this peculiar moment. Briefly imagined writing the scenario up and sending it off to Ann Landers, see what her take on it was. Without being able to defer to her refined guidance, Pony went with his loudest instinct and hid. Sort of. Stuck his head down between his knees anyway. Deep down he knew it was silly, stinky and a bit like an ostrich putting its head in the sand, but at least he avoided a water-cooler conversation about the weather. While Blitz had the good grace of a worldly European, and passed without a word, Pony wasn't so lucky with the rest of them.

The shelter emptied out in surprising short order. As hikers filed past, each acknowledged Pony in their own way. Shaggy Bob grinned and Giggles giggled. The Crying Hawaiian stopped to complain about the day's impending climbs. Lazy JoJo gave him a straight-faced nod and Bartleby grunted distractedly. When Wham-O came through, he couldn't resist—he actually flicked his frisbee to Pony. It landed on the postman's lap.

❦ ❦ ❦

Register: Cosby Knob Shelter

4/24 VARMIN ALERT: Spent the last 20 minutes
      watching a stripe-backed chim-punk circle the food
      bags. The little scamp has evolved to where the
      bear cables are no longer an obstacle. He went up,
      over and right down to the food bags. Got dizzy
      watching him zip back & forth. Now he's sitting
      there on the damn food bag, chillin' like the Little
      Prince on his planetoid.   - Bawdy
      P.S. varmint + vermin = varmin

Midafternoon on Easter Sunday. It was clear and cheery; altogether a great day for walking down out of the Smoky Mountains. Bawdy was some miles ahead and Coyote a little ways behind. Skunkers and Flutterby walked side-by-side, enjoying the downhill cruise and talking about whatever came to mind.

"—comes over before church and gives her a present. Cardboard box about this big, all wrapped up with a bow on it, right? Turns out he got her a baby bunny. White with a little gray patch over its left eye. About the size of your fist. I guess he'd ordered a cage for it, but it hadn't come in yet. So we put a book on the box top to weight it down and trooped off to church. Came back two hours later to find our three cats lined up and chowing on the carcass like a pride of lions. Not much left but a couple of feet and some fur."

"That's awful," Flutterby said.

"Oh yeah it was. My sister starts crying, disappears to her

room and my mother makes me clean it all up. Couldn't look at those cats the same way again."

An oldish woman hiked towards them, a walking stick in one hand, an Easter basket swinging in the other.

"Happy Easter," she called. "You two thru-hiking?"

"Yes, ma'am."

"Well good, I've got some treats for ya. Easter eggs, jelly beans and Rice Krispy squares."

"Hmmmm," Skunkers grinned, "sounds good."

"Which would you like?"

"All, I guess," he said. When Flutterby elbowed him, he quickly added, "But anything would be great, ma'am."

The old woman pursed her lips, "Let's see now. I got two last bundles of jelly beans left, so you each get one of those. Looks like three Rice Krispies, and one hard-boiled egg." She puzzled over what do and finally asked, "Are there a lot of hikers coming along behind you?"

"No, ma'am," Skunkers cheerfully replied. "Probably not anyone else coming this way today."

The old woman hesitated. It was easy to see she wasn't quite ready to run out of Easter treats yet. "Well," she said, "I guess you can take it all. You do see anyone, you'll be sure to share, won't you?"

"Yes, ma'am," Skunkers beamed. He'd already snorked one square into his mouth, but managed to fit a muffled "Thank you" out around it.

"Thanks," Flutterby called after her.

Skunkers choked down the first square, "Want half the egg?"

"I don't like them or Rice Krispy treats. I'll take your jelly beans though."

Wasn't too terribly long before Coyote came hurrying up and out of breath, "That old woman said she gave you the last of her trail magic, but that you were supposed to share."

Skunkers' mouth was already distended full of hard-boiled egg and the second Rice Krispy treat, but still he quick made room for the third treat. "Sorry, dude," he said around the grotesque mouthful, "We thought you were up ahead or something."

"You left me eating lunch at that last shelter. And you knew I was right behind you, because my last words to you were, 'I'll be right behind you.' Where are the jelly beans at least? You gonna bogart them too?"

Flutterby shrugged guiltily, held her hand out. "Only got the black ones left. Want them?"

"No, I don't want seven nasty-ass black jelly beans," Coyote snapped. "Why do they even make black jelly beans? Everybody hates them." He hesitated, "Okay, gimme the black jelly beans. Maybe they're not as bad as I remember."

He tasted one, grimaced, swallowed.

"Not so bad, right?"

"Worse actually," he groused. Though that didn't stop him from popping the next one into his mouth.

Register: Groundhog Creek Shelter

4/25   It's been nine days now
       since I changed undies—oh,
       the humanity!

                        High-Ku

❦ ❦ ❦

The climb up to the summit of Max Patch was more relentlessly steady than ruthlessly steep, but still it was long and punishing. A rising straightaway that went on and on like the standard ethics lecture from Coyote's father—a stuffed-shirt of a lawyer-man if ever there was one. There was no water, no variety and, since the leaf cover was just starting to come in, no shady spots for a decent break.

Bawdy called back over his shoulder, "Got any water left?"

Coyote didn't answer. His throat was so dry, it hurt to swallow. The dark rings around his eyes and cracked lips were early indicators of dehydration. At the last water source, a sign had said the water was point-two off trail, down into a gulley. They'd opted to keep going, figured they could hold out for something closer to the AT. Funny how Coyote didn't blink at the prospect of hiking from Georgia to Maine, but no way was he going point-two out of his way to fill his water bladder from some drippy little mud hole. Hell, it could've been glacier melt served up in a goddamn goblet and he wouldn't have gone. Two-tenths of a mile was more than a thousand feet. More than three football fields. Except, you had to factor in the return trip too. Make it six football fields worth of walking, all of it going down and back up a treacherously steep incline. As Bawdy liked to say—no way, hombre. Long as he could remember, Coyote'd been a gambler. He'd rather take his chances. Would much rather lose on a roll of the dice or the turn of a card, than not gamble at all.

Well, he'd got his wish. And he and Bawdy had both clearly lost this round.

Back at that last water, he'd had maybe two or three mouthfuls left splashing in the bottom of his water bottle. Was already running a couple quarts low—could feel his tongue beginning to swell and a headache coming on. Now, five miles later, his mouth was choking full of tongue while his head did a passable impression of a rotten coconut. Felt like it could split open any time.

Ahead, Bawdy was sucking at his drinking hose. Made that slurping straw noise from the bottom of a milkshake. He stopped and turned, specks of white spittle at the corners of his mouth, "I'm out."

"I've been empty for the last mile."

Bawdy shook his head, commiserating and trying to clear his mind at the same time. Despite the exertion, his face was pale. Looked like he might swoon.

"This sucks," he whined. "Makes ya wish we'd gone off for water back there, huh?"

Coyote stuck Bawdy with his hiking pole. Not hard, but enough to prod him along, get him moving again. No point in standing around, moaning about water. Had to keep on, assume there was some around the next bend, over the next rise, down the next mountain.

"Not a chance," Coyote said, "I wouldn't change a thing. You can't win without losing."

"What," Bawdy wheezed, "the hell does that mean?"

"I like winning so much, I don't mind losing. Can't really have one without the other. I'll pick my poison, take my chances—and there'll be no complaining or second-guessing afterwards—win or lose. Course, that being said, I would happily pay three hundred bucks for a pint of cold water right now."

After another twenty minutes of steady progress, they came upon an old man sleeping trailside. Octogenarian, easy. Had greasy gray hair, a long wispy beard and eyebrows like maybe the world's two oldest, woolliest caterpillars had up and died there on his face. Laying back amidst a throng of wildflowers and shin-high grasses, his head resting on a clunky old external-frame pack.

A Great Dane, murky tiger-stripes scattered over a tawny hide, lazed a few yards beyond the sleeping hiker. One black ear perked up, tracking their arrival. From out of the dog's closed mouth, a single yellow butterfly wing was visible. Far as Coyote could see, the damned thing was still flapping.

The old guy's eyes were closed; he looked peaceful as any dozen angels.

First thought that flashed across Coyote's mind: If this crust is dead, I'm gonna drink the hell out of his water. "He breathing?"

"I don't know, Yote. Why don't you stick *him* with your pole."

The dog high-stepped towards them on long, spindly legs. Covered about half the distance and sniffed the air before whuffing at them curiously. This wasn't remotely aggressive or even loud, but still it woke the little old guy.

His eyes were sparkling sharp and a shade of green Coyote had never seen before—somewhere between pine and kelly. The oldster stretched big and yawned bigger. When the yawned finally wound down, he grinned at them like a hungry goblin.

"You feeling alright, man?"

The dog turned and started licking the guy's face. "Heh-

heh," he chuckled. "Heh-heh."

"Sorry to wake you, dude," Coyote said. "We thought you might be having some trouble."

"Trouble? What trouble?" The old guy hopped up quick as a cat, but without any of the balance or surefootedness. He sort of wambled sideways before catching himself against a tree trunk. From which, he gave them a long looking over.

"You boys hungry?"

"Shit yeah, we are," Bawdy said, a smile cracking across his face for the first time in hours.

"Good, good. I got something you're gonna like."

Coyote couldn't help himself—his eyes opened wide and his grin stretched tight. He took a step forward. The sudden possibility of an unexpected bounty, the kindness of a stranger at a time like this was—well, he'd been hearing about trail magic pretty much since Springer, but hadn't personally experienced any yet. For a can of warm soda, Coyote would've carried this guy's pack all the way to Damascus.

The old guy pulled something from a back pocket. Looked to be an old book with a badly curled cover. He slapped the thing into Bawdy's outstretched hands. Bawdy read the title aloud, "The Petersen Field Guide to Edible Plants of Eastern & Central North America."

"Go over that way about forty, fifty yards," the old guy pointed a bony finger down along a steep westward slope. "There's a whole feast waiting for you. Wild garlic, Solomon's Seal, ramps, white trillium—all kinds of stuff. Fill you right up."

He followed that pronouncement with a beamingly sincere smile, like he'd just handed over a couple of New York strips, medium-rare and still steaming.

"Lettuce?" Coyote snorted. His headache, momentarily forgotten, thundered back to the forefront. He gave the old man a withering look and started walking again.

"Wasn't quite what I imagine when people talk about trail magic," Bawdy admitted when he caught up.

"That wasn't magic," Coyote growled, "that was just mean."

Shortly before the sun went down on Deer Park Mountain Shelter, they started a little campfire to celebrate their impending arrival into Hot Springs. Just three more easy miles. Being that Hot Springs was the first trail town the AT actually travelled through, this seemed like a big deal and worthy of a fire.

Ella showed up as the first flames were crackling to life.

She put the damper on the festivities quick as a cold spring rain. In the first fifteen minutes, she incorrectly corrected Skunkers (he'd been right in what he'd been saying), interrupted a story Pork Chop was telling (about a time he hit a bear with his car) and started in pecking at Flutterby.

"What day did you start?" she wanted to know.

"April third."

"Did you hike the Approach Trail?"

"Yeah. Me and Bawdy spent the night up on Springer together. Remember that big, beefy guy with the hat? He talked so much I was hiding in my hammock by six o'clock."

Bawdy started to say something, but Ella cut him off.

"You're doing good, huh? Moving right along."

"I don't know, I guess so," Flutterby shrugged. "Happy to still be out here, anyway."

"I started on the eleventh, so my mileage is, you know, better than yours, but still, "that's cool," she said. Turned then, and without taking a breath, started in on Coyote, "So officially, Yote—that beard of yours is coming in like pubes on a ten-year-old."

This caught him flat-footed and off balance. To be fair, his mouth was puffed full with hot, cheesy beans and rice, but even after swallowing, he had nothing, or at least no barbed comeback that wasn't *too* sharp. Used to be he happily erred on the side of drawing lots of blood, but he learned to see the flaws in that strategy during his four year stint at Morgantown, in West Virginia. It may have been a minimum-security joint, mostly hosting the white collar criminal set, but it still wasn't the kind of place you went around verbally assaulting fellow prisoners without suffering repercussions.

He settled on this eye-rolling, head-shaking, nostril-flaring, please-god-if-you-won't-hit-her-with-a-bolt-of-lightning-at-least-send-one-for-me look at Bawdy. Bawdy bounce-passed the look on to Skunkers, Skunkers alley-ooped it to Flutterby who fired it over to Pork Chop. Pork Chop wanted to give it to Squirtz, but Squirtz had disappeared off to the privy yet again, so he had to settle for Old Man Trouble. Of course Trouble wasn't paying attention and he was at least half-deaf, so it pretty much died there.

Like all the best forces of nature, Ella was both overwhelming and oblivious to all else. As destructive and domineering as a red haired class five twister. And just like when a funnel cloud tears across tornado alley, the only option was to hunker low and hope she passed by without leaving too much wreckage in her wake.

Took no time at all for people to drift away to bed.

Left alone at the fire, Ella turned on her phone, "It is so nice to be out of the Smokies," she said to no one in particular, "I couldn't get a signal up there to save my life."

❦

Sometime later, Coyote lay on his stomach in his sleeping bag. By the red glowing coals of the fire, it was easy to make out Ella's silhouette. And even easier to hear her talking on her phone.

"—oh, I love Kanye West. Even though he's a complete douche. You know, for giving Taylor Swift that smack down. But like, I hate her too, so—"

Immediately to Coyote's right, Bawdy was fast asleep with his head pointed into the shelter. After popping an Ambien and putting his ear buds in, he was out in no time. Flutterby was on the far side of Bawdy, with her head facing towards the fire.

"How much longer before her battery runs out?" she whispered. Coyote had to lean over Bawdy's feet to hear her.

"What?"

"Guess she's gonna talk until her battery goes dead. How much longer, d'ya think?"

"With that stupid solar charger, there's no saying how much juice she's got."

"—not yet. This one guy definitely likes me, but he's kind

of a, you know, a squinty-eyed, egg-head dorko with food-stains on his shirt. Thinks he's all witty, but he's a wanna-be-funny-poser—"

"She's talking about Bawdy now."

"—no, I'm pretty much the fastest chick on the trail. They're all too worried about breaking a nail or getting dirty to push the big miles—"

"I'm starting to hate that Patagucci hoochie."

Flutterby nodded, "I've been trying really hard not to."

"—what? Can you hear me now? Yeah, you keep cutting out. My reception sucks. This phone is so annoying—"

Max Patch was the king of all the grassy balds. The one bald to rule them all. It reached up to more than 4,600 feet above sea level, but like the tip of an iceberg, only the top bit was actually visible. And that top bit looked little more than a low grassy dome. It was bucolic, like something from a pastoral watercolor or maybe straight out of the Shire.

Bartleby was alone when he reached the summit. Pony and the rest must've already gone ahead to the next shelter. After flumping down amidst the tall grasses, he removed his boots and socks. Slugged water and took in the panoramic view. He could see fifty miles in every direction, easy. Except that he couldn't really. On a clear day, sure, but this wasn't one of those. Wispy white clouds blotched out much of the northern horizon. To the southwest, the Smokies were hidden beneath a high stacked cairn of purple storm clouds. These promised serious rain. For the moment at least, the whole of the dome was bathed in sunlight that seemed somehow both hotter and brighter than usual.

Bartleby leaned against his pack with a blank mind and an empty soul. He lost track of time until something tickled the bottom of his foot. Felt like a blade of grass or maybe an ant. A few minutes later, something else, a fly probably, landed on his cheek. He felt it walk through the wild scruff of his beard and climb the bridge of his nose. A chilly gust blew through, sent a shiver up his legs. He leaned back out of the worst of it.

He stared up into a bright blue emptiness and felt the sun warm his bones.

And then a niggling little thought took shape in his heretofore blank mind.

Maybe this was exactly where he was supposed to be.

This thought of his was actually one of Angie's favorite sayings. An old standby, a catch-all panacea and fatalistic write-off for everything that was happening at any given moment. For the first five years they were together, he simply ignored it. When the housing market imploded and shit started flying at the family fan, Bartleby heard it too often to do anything but hate it. Got this zinc-y mouthful of nails taste in his throat whenever she said it. When the dust began to settle after the collapse, he stopped listening to what people were saying, which included Angie and that "where we are is exactly where we need to be" mantra of hers. And now, he was lying out on the top of some grassy dome he'd never heard of before in his life, wondering if just maybe somehow he was actually on the right track.

One of the least enjoyable aspects of thru-hiking involved pooping in the woods. This was an inevitable undertaking for long-distance hikers, and one that certainly took some getting used to.

There were two fundamental issues to consider: comfort and privacy.

The quick hitters didn't have to worry so much about comfort. They were in and out well before thigh muscles could start up quivering with fatigue. It was the slow and steady shitters, the people who liked to sit contemplatively or browse the Lifestyle section before things got rolling, that were most inconvenienced by the absence of a toilet on which to hunker.

Flutterby was the quickest of the quick hitters. She preferred going in the woods to the stench and ugliness that were quintessential characteristics of any self-respecting privy.

The default position was the hover. A knees bent, ass in the air stance with shoulders hunched forward. Imagine a downhill skier without pants. At the best of times, hovering wasn't any kind of fun. A full on squat was much more natural and comfortable, but of course, squatting wasn't exactly an easy thing to accomplish with one's pants still looped around both ankles. And with hiking boots on, it required an act of congress for most hikers to kick a foot free of its corresponding pant leg.

Bartleby learned to hold onto a nearby tree trunk for support. Took some pressure off his already exhausted leg muscles. Being an exceptional athlete, Skunkers had the balance and grace to hold a deep squat without bothering to remove his pants.

With two previous thru-hikes under his belt, Old Man Trouble was both literally and figuratively an "old" hand at going in the woods. While he hiked, he kept an eye peeled for likely little spots with at least some privacy and, preferably, a horizontal tree limb or a downed trunk over which he could perch.

Privacy was the other serious concern. Contrary to common logic, there wasn't as much privacy to be had out there in the woods as one might assume. When the trail was wandering down through the lowlands, the surrounding terrain was often marshy wet or briared over so as only to be passable at high cost. At high elevations, jutting rocks and steep pitches often kept hikers traveling along a narrow corridor. Hikers could either hold out for better pickings or do their best to hover, hide and hope like hell nobody came along for a bit.

Coyote called this getting caught "brown-handed." As often as it happened to him, he'd earned the right to name it. Like all other aspects of his life, Coyote preferred rolling the dice over a sure bet. He would pass perfectly fine spots in the woods on the hopes that he could make it to the next privy in time. He was often successful, but when he wasn't, he was frequently left with little choice but to go behind shrubs that made Charlie Brown's Christmas tree look robust.

The midlands were the sweet spot. They generally offered room enough for hikers to roam a hundred yards off trail, find a nice copse of trees or a good view and get down to it. Of course, bushwhacking two hundred yards (there and back again) however many times a day, wasn't exactly an ideal way to spend time and energy. Though it was a great way to stumble through a ground nest of wasps, upset a sunning snake or otherwise have a negative interaction with the natural world.

Lazy JoJo was lucky. From her days driving truck, she'd developed a gut of steel. Didn't have to go more than once every other day or so, and even that was negotiable. Miraculously, she managed to reach a privy all but two or three times the entire hike.

All of their eating coupled with limited access to traditional bathroom facilities made thru-hikers a demographic ripe for various intestinal difficulties. Once, after hoovering a fourteen inch Dagwood-style hoagie, Bawdy was dismayed to see blood in his stool. Started to get nervous, thought he'd somehow contracted a hike ending case of giardia. On closer inspection, he realized it wasn't blood, but simply undigested red peppers.

Squirtz popped Imodium tablets like they were Flintstone vitamins. While this helped regulate some of his irregularities, it also gave him pistachio ice cream colored poop.

Two-Speed Tortoise couldn't hit a cat-hole if her life depended on it. More than not she had to use a stick after the fact.

Being German, Blitz wasn't familiar with the English adage about shit rolling downhill. If he had been, he likely wouldn't have set up shop facing downhill on a steep slope while wearing nothing more than flip-flops.

Bawdy and Skunkers were having a sprawling conversation about television programs they'd both watched or wanted to watch or hadn't yet watched and what they thought of them, if anything at all.

Coyote watched next to no television himself (unless dog races counted), and found this discussion boring at best. After a few miles, it became largely intolerable. So he interrupted. "Well, I guess the real question is: which one's your favorite? Black or blue?"

"Favorite what?"

"What're you talking about black or blue?"

Coyote just kept hiking and let them think about it for a while.

Skunkers might never have figured it out, but it only took Bawdy a minute or two, "You're talking about Flutterby's sport-bras, right? I don't know—the blue one, I guess."

"Yep," Skunkers agreed, "definitely the blue one."

"Two votes for Blueberry Hills. Personally, I'm a fan of Black Beauties."

"You named her bras? That's weirdo-creepy, man."

"Not cool, dude."

Pause.

"You got a name for Tortoise's bra?"

"Ripe Tomatoes."

"Giggles?"

"Sweet Peas."

"How about Lazy JoJo?"

"Yeah, I'm calling that one Barney."

❦ ❦ ❦

The morning after Lazy JoJo threatened to make him cry,

the Original Grand Poohbah picked up his pace. He hadn't really liked hanging around with any of those stupid newbs and something about the way JoJo carried herself made him think she maybe could make do on her threat. Hell, her ugly leer-of-a-smile was almost enough to do the job. He dropped it down into second gear and left the smell of burning sneaker sole behind him. Easiest thing in the world for an old pro like himself. Wasn't nothing but a thought to push on a little further each day. The extra miles added up quick as anything. He shot through the last half of the Smokies, started skimming along towards Hot Springs.

Would have been nice to spend more time on top of Max Patch, but sometimes you had to make sacrifices. Poohbah was pleased when he pulled into an empty Walnut Mountain Shelter. From there, it was an easy thirteen mile cruise down to town. The plan was to get up with the birds and bang the miles out early—hit Hot Springs no later than 11 o'clock. Slurp down a greasy-hot meal at the Smoky Mountain Diner, pick up mail, resupply at the Dollar General, maybe scam a shower, wring out his clothes and keep on marching right out of town. Just a mile or two beyond would be enough. Slow as they all hiked, he knew he'd probably be okay taking a zero-mile day in Hot Springs, but better safe than sorry. He really didn't want to see JoJo again. Besides, that Flutterby chick was probably only a day or so ahead. He grinned at the thought of hiking around her for a while. Maybe he'd be able to work his magic and get loved up like he had way back in '97.

And the rain that had been making threatening promises all day long, somehow, improbably, didn't make good on those threats until he was setup safe and dry inside the shelter. He couldn't help but grin a little wider.

The final bit of good news—since he'd gone faster than expected and gained ground so precipitously, Poohbah's food bag still had a pleasant heft. In addition to the evening's packet of Stove Top Savory Herb stuffing, it contained an odd bagel, half a block of muenster, the final third of a hard pepperoni, plenty of dry-roasted peanuts, and even a handful of soy jerky. It would be his solemn responsibility to make sure that none of it reached Hot Springs intact.

As he started preparing dinner, Poohbah's grin threatened to split his face. Was pretty much stuck there until he looked up and saw Blitz bearing down on him. The kid was all gangly-footed and smiling when he reached the shelter. Took a seat, shook some of the water from his head.

"Dry shelter ez good, ja?"

And he was only the front-runner. Over the next few hours, Pony Express, Lazy JoJo and Bartleby followed him in.

❧

It was late and dark. To be more precise, it was very late and really dark and windy and wet to boot. And cold as a witch's you know what. A not-so-distant boom of thunder woke Pony. He rolled over, tried to get comfortable. Which was, he'd come to understand, pretty much impossible on hard shelter floors. But what they lacked in luxury they made up for in weatherproofness. Course, he was more than willing to trade a little luxury for the privilege of being out of the worst of it on a night like this.

The wind was driving the rain down fierce. Tat-tat-tatting

185

against the shelter's tin roof. Loud sure, but somehow not loud enough to drown out the ragged-jagged consumptive-sounding snores slipping from Bartleby's open mouth. Without really trying, Pony could pick out Blitz's whuff-snort and Lazy JoJo's distinctly cyclical gnort-pooooos. Even Poohbah was in on it tonight, a rho–rho–rho–rho–rho slowly building and building until finally being released in a low euwwww, like air leaking out of an inner tube.

Luckily, Pony snagged one of the end spots. Sleeping on the end, up against a side-wall, meant he wasn't surrounded by snorers or kickers or encroached upon too badly if and when the shelter filled up. *Especially* when the shelter filled up. Out in the middle of a full shelter you were just as likely to pass the night sleeping on your neighbor's pad as your own. Pony felt like the end spots afforded him a modicum of control and comfort. Only half the neighbors to contend with.

He rolled onto his belly and watched as the wind-whipped mist blew past the shelter opening. Thought about starting a letter to his mother, but didn't feel like rooting through his pack for pen and paper. Thought about eating a tortilla with cheese and mustard and maybe some tuna, but couldn't see his way to sorting through the confusion of food bags hanging from the rafter like so many bunched grapes.

After a time, Pony's eyes started to glaze over. Just as he shifted to his side to resume the battle for sleep something out in the woods caught his eye.

A little bobbing flicker of light. Sometimes it was obvious, but then it disappeared for long moments. When it reappeared it was always closer than he expected. He lay there, fish-gaping, as the light grew to what he finally recognized as the cold

LED glow of a headlamp.

Fifty yards and then fifty feet. Fifteen. Five.

And just there in the darkness behind the light, a little man. A big external frame pack on his back and beside him, a dog. Despite the saddlebags lashed over the dog's back, Pony instantly recognized the silhouette as belonging to a Great Dane. Both man and dog were soaked through and dripping wet.

The little man came to a stop just under the roof eave; the dog's leash grasped in one hand, a knobby black walking staff in the other. The man played his light across the shelter's interior. It was blinding bright. He left it shining directly into Pony's eyes.

"Oh-wee, boy. You got room for two more, sonny?"

"Sure," Pony sputtered, "sure." Then, "Someone else coming behind?"

The little man spun around, pointing his headlamp back into the dark. "I don't know. Ya see someone?"

"No, no. You said there were two of you."

"Oh," he said. "Heh. I meant Jane and me."

"Jane?"

Hearing her name called, the Great Dane leapt onto the shelter platform. Tall stilt legs scrabbled for purchase, pointy ears quivered excitedly and a collar bell tinkled madly. She, Jane, the dog, took a few steps closer to Pony, the postman. He retreated until his back was against the shelter sidewall. She had to step on his legs (still tangled in his sleeping bag) to bring her face in close to his.

To clarify, she didn't *have* to. No one was making her, no one was prompting or encouraging her even, but she did bring her face close to Pony's. And to do so, she *had* to put wet paws onto his legs, consequently getting mud and damp all over Pony's sleeping bag and his soft self.

Pony wasn't worried about the sudden influx of moisture in his personal space. Hadn't yet occurred to him as a problem worth considering. He was staring, stiff and scared, at the huge canine countenance looming before him. Cliché or no, Pony Express, fresh off a twenty-year stint with the United States Postal Service, had a long standing dread of dogs.

You work two decades delivering mail and you're going to have some canine encounters. And some of those are going to be real whoppers. Tree climbing, shoe losing affairs that could still set your heart to thumping fifteen years later, if ever those memories run loose in your mind.

Postmaster Lou Griggins, Pony's boss and uncle, called it "contact." As in enemy contact. "More contact on route six again, huh? Crap bastards are getting bold. Time we pushed back a little, eh?" From a locked desk drawer Lou would pull a tall, pressurized spray can. There was an image of a cloven-hoofed and crimson-horned devil blowing flames from its mouth on the side of the can. Above the devilish image, in a flowing red script, the words "El Aliento del Diablo." Which translated roughly to Satan's Spit. Some special brand of pepper spray his uncle imported from a tiny village outside of Oaxaca, Mexico. "Give them a taste of hell for me," he'd gruff. There was a practiced cadence to this phrase and its delivery that always made Pony think it was something Lou had said to his men as they soldiered deep into the bowels of a Vietnamese jungle.

Jane paused there, an inch or so from Pony's face. So close he could make out individual drops of water streaming down her black muzzle en route to her bristly chin. Jane sniffed at him once, twice and snorted through flared nostrils. If all that wasn't already too much, too casually close, too informally intrusive for Pony's pleasure, she presumed to lick a thick tongue over a fair portion of his face.

After which, she barked once, a single sharp exclamation loud enough to wake most anyone still sleeping.

"Wha'zat?" Bartleby mumbled.

Lazy JoJo shot up, "What's happening?"

"Stuff it over there," Poohbah grumbled.

"Whuff-snort," Blitz continued seamlessly.

Sensing a conversational lull, Jane seized the opportunity and gave herself a shake. It was a frenzied thing starting at her nose, but quickly spreading to encompass rubbery black lips, pointed ears, saggy shoulder skin, staunch hindquarters and a whip-like tail. Like most Great Danes, Jane was a big dog, and her shake was sized to match. Water flung clear across the shelter, soaking everyone and everything in a fine spray.

This produced a general outcry, at which the little man with the headlamp only chuckled.

"Now, where will we be the least botheration to you?" he asked.

Lazy JoJo and Bartleby quick scuttled over towards Blitz and Poohbah on the far side of the shelter. This unintentionally but effectively cut Pony off and left him behind.

The little man proceeded to shuck and hang wet clothes and spread out into the space provided.

Various headlamps were partially illuminating the shelter's interior and by that light, Pony got his first look at the little man. He was certainly old and he had some trouble wrestling his wet shirt over his head. When he finally managed it though, he looked crinkled and wrinkled, knobbily sunken and gleamingly pale. He wore what looked like a leather aviator's cap on his head and, despite having removed his shirt, he was still wearing Red Baron-style flight goggles. One of the lens looked cracked and both were steamed up and rain streaked.

"Now where did my headlamp get to," he muttered, rifling through pockets and gear.

"It's on your head," Pony said.

The man felt around on his head.

"So it is," he chuckled. When he removed the headlamp, goggles and cap, loose strands of fine white hair fell down to his shoulders. A long, sharp nose set off his face, accentuated by a pointed beard the color of dirty snow. His pack was a clankingly cumbersome thing with various bits of gear hanging down and swaying crazily to-and-fro. He wore knee-high gaiters and massive boots that made hearty sucking noises when they came off his wrinkled, white feet.

"I'm known as the Mad Hatter. On account of all my hats and my work as a haberdasher. This is my trusted sidekick, familiar and animal compatriot, Sweet Jane the Greatest Dane. We're sorry to bother you at this hour. Lost track of time, one thing led to another and lo and behold, here we are, strolling into the shelter later than expected."

He seemed to be addressing all of this specifically at Pony, though in a volume that could be heard way over by the privy.

"D'ya know that wives' tale about mushrooms coming out during a thunderstorm? When we heard the first rumble we said it's time to see if there's any meat on that bone. I might look old and Jane doesn't look too terribly nimble, but we can still pounce when pouncing's called for. Away into the under-brush, turning over stones, rooting round under logs.

"We couldn't find a single one. After a couple of hours, it dawned on us that maybe the wives' tale spoke of rain, and not thunder, as the impetus for the mushroom's flowering. I mean—mushrooms must not have ears for a reason, right?

"So we've solved half the riddle, as it were. Mushrooms aren't called out by the thunder. And now all that's left us is to wait for the proper moment when a soggy, sodden deluge dumps down and then we'll verify whether or not they actually come out in the rain."

He finished off by flashing a bright smile around at his collected audience. There was a long pause, a pregnant moment of awe to which Blitz' response was likely as good as any other.

"Whuff-snort."

"But...it's raining now," said Pony.

"Gotta take a leak," grumbled Lazy JoJo.

"Mad Chatter's more like it," Poohbah mumbled.

"Heh-heh, heh-heh," was Mad Chatter's only reply. He pulled a thermal shirt on and shined his light around the shelter. "Since there are no ladies present, would anyone protest if I changed right here?"

Lazy JoJo had shrugged into a waterproof shell and was standing down off the platform, no more than a foot from Mad Chatter. "There's a lady right here, but this lady would squirt off the edge if y'all weren't so squeamish. Go ahead, old man. Promise you: wrinkled, warty and wet—I seen it all before."

With that, she splashed off into the dark.

"Now that," Mad Chatter nodded approvingly, "is some

lady."

"Twice the man I am," Pony agreed, "on my best days."

Mad Chatter proceeded to remove his pants. Since he was still standing, he had some difficulty getting the tangle of wet legs off over his feet. This accomplished, he cast about, bare-bottomed and goose-pimpled, for a peg to hang them on. Finally, with more grunting and flailing about than one might have expected, he managed to wiggle an old pair of quilted long johns up and over the wilted cock dangling down beneath the flannel hem of his shirt.

"Again, fellow men of the woods, let me apologize. This time for my lengthy nakedness. Take it from an expert, getting old is not easy at the best of times, and this," he paused to check the time on his watch, "can't possibly be the best of times. At least that poor woman wasn't subjected to my fumbled shortcomings."

"Actually," JoJo said from inside her sleeping bag, "I've been back for most of it. And from this perspective at least, you've got no shortcomings to apologize for."

Pony was still sitting up, curled tight to the wall. Try as he might, he couldn't quite avoid Jane. Soon as Mad Chatter had started talking, she knowingly lay right down in the space vacated by JoJo and Bartleby. Since then Jane had been gradually inching closer and closer, surreptitiously encroaching upon Pony's scant sleep space. Now her head was resting on his pad and her body was leaned up against his leg.

"Er... ah," Pony started. "Your dog—"

"Seems to have taken a liking to you, young man. I can assure you, Sweet Jane doesn't just go to anyone, but only to those she deems worthy. And a more loyal friend you'll not find out in these or any other woods."

"But, I'm—er, I don't...."

The old man upended his pack and sent an eclectic jumble of gear tumbling out. Now," he said, "what have I done with that—"

"We're trying to sleep here, Chatter," Poohbah started. "Seriously, you gotta stuff it up tight—"

"—whiskey of mine. Heh-heh, here it is. Interest anyone in a nightcap?"

"Well, since we're up," Poohbah said. He reached across for the flask and took a stiff belt before passing it to Bartleby, who didn't care for any late night whiskey but tried to give it to Pony and couldn't reach, so instead Bartleby handed it to Lazy JoJo who could reach and when she didn't pass it back quickly enough, Poohbah snatched it from her for another glug.

"Heh-heh," said Chatter. He was preparing to cook, "Once a long time ago, back when I was fresh to the haberdashery business, the hat game, as I've come to call it, I met a woman. Had a perfectly oval head, which, by the by, is much less common than you'd ever think—"

"Frak. Battlestar."

"Frick."

"Florg. Legion of Super Heroes."

"Fargin'. Johnny Dangerously."

"Frell. Farscape.

"Phunk. Black Eyed Peas."

"Fierfek. Star Wars: Republic Commando."

"What the hell is that?"

"A video game."

"Jesus—Ella was right on the money, huh?"

"Yeah? How's that?"

"You really are a squinty-eyed, egg-headed dorko."

End to end, downtown Hot Springs was maybe a mile long. The AT mostly followed Bridge Street through the drowsy heart of the little town. It eventually passed over Spring Creek, railroad tracks and the French Broad River before slipping back into the woods. Establishments of note: a budget motor inn, a gear shop, a public library full to bursting with friendly librarians and internet terminals, The Smoky Mountain Diner, a Dollar General, a happy-to-help-you post office and a little bar with a covered deck off the back. Squeezed in between the French Broad and the train tracks was a dingy laundromat and an RV campground that let hikers tent for cheap.

"This place is pretty much perfect, huh?"

"I guess." Bawdy transferred clothes from the washer to the dryer. He hadn't much considered it.

"Seriously," Coyote kept on, "the locals couldn't be friendlier. Look, this morning I had my first bowl of grits and now I'm sitting here at the end of town knee-deep in a six-pack and ain't nobody blinking an eye at me."

"Guess that's one definition of perfect."

"Whatever, Grumpsy. Don't be a hater just cuz you got laundry duty again. Not my fault you can't Rock-Paper-Scissor for shit."

"You got anything better to do than harass me while I'm cleaning your stanky-ass clothes?"

Coyote worked through a mental checklist, "Already picked up my maildrop, resupplied, showered, perused the gear shop, porked down a nice big breakfast/ lunch and now," he held up the bottle, "I'm curing blisters with beer. So, no, I guess I don't got nothing better to do."

He offered over a fresh bottle and grinned.

Bawdy took the beer, "Listen, I gotta call home, so why don't you go bother Skunkers for a while."

Coyote slunk to the door, "I can tell when I'm not wanted."

"Now you just gotta learn to leave whenever you get that feeling."

❦

Truth was, Bawdy lost RPS on purpose. He liked doing laundry. Enjoyed the whole process from start to finish. Found it to be soothing. He always brought a book, but sometimes it was enough to just sit and listen to the lumpy thump-thump of clothes going around the washer or the steady rhythm of them tumbling dry. Loved that springy smell of clean clothes and the comforting glow of warmth when they first came out the dryer. And he particularly enjoyed folding them afterwards. He popped life back into Skunkers' booney hat. Paired like socks and tucked them together. Shook his shorts out, pushed the pockets back through. Took special care with Flutterby's unmentionables, not untoward interest as much as a gentle reverence. He handled Coyote's union-suit with less care, but still hand-pressed it free of wrinkles before folding and stacking it with the rest.

Took the folded pile in his arms and set off back down Bridge Street. As he went past, he saw that Skunkers, Coyote and Squirtz were bellied up at the bar, a place called Rock Bottom. He kept on, almost reached the motel room, when Ella appeared out of nowhere. She still wore her backpack and a fine layer of trail dust.

"Are you staying here at the motor lodge?"

"Uh-huh." He didn't stop or even slow, kept on heading for his room.

"Is it nice?"

"It's a motor lodge. Do they even try for nice?"

"Can I check out your room? See if it's okay?"

He arrived at his door, fumbled with the key. "I guess, sure."

Damp tents and sleeping bags were draped over lamp shades and headboards. Water bottles and titanium cookware and the contents of maildrops exploded out everywhere. A careful soul could barely take a step without tripping over a pack or groceries or stinking hiking boots. An ooze of used towels spilled from the bathroom.

"A little cluttered, but you get the idea."

Ella dropped her pack, plopped down on one of the beds and stretched back. "Feels so good to sit down for a minute, you know?"

❧

"It's really not that big a deal," Skunkers said.

"Course it is, you bumpkin. She can't stay in our room."

"With only the two beds, it's already weird sharing with Flutterby, and she's a decent human being," Bawdy said.

"With a great ass," Coyote added. "I mean, is it me or is she hotter than a spoonful of heroin?"

They were sitting around a table in the bar, empty beer bottles littering the tabletop. Dead soldiers, Skunkers called them.

"So go tell Ella to scram."

"You think I didn't? She just kept unpacking. Then she took the last clean towel, started undressing—"

"That was mine," Skunkers moaned. "I was saving it for the morning."

"—and I came running straight here. You know, before she made me wash her feet or something. I mean, the girl's a nut. A ginger-headed nut."

"Jesus."

"God."

"Amen." Coyote shook his head, stood up, "Girl's like a bad case of nut bugs. We ain't never getting rid of her."

"Where you going?"

"Get more beer. Only way everyone survives the night."

❧

When Shaggy Bob stopped over for a drink he got right to the latest gossip, "You hear about Again? Tore his meniscus. Went off at Newfound Gap."

"Again?" said Bawdy.

"Again," Shaggy Bob nodded.

"Again?" said Skunkers. "What happened again at Newfound Gap?"

"What happened to Again at Newfound Gap," Shaggy Bob corrected him.

"Agren," Coyote mumbled. He was head down on the table and all but unconscious.

"The guy's cursed. Should give it up already, get on with his life."

Shaggy Bob lit a new cigarette from his old one, "I don't know. I mean, maybe it's all about the journey and not about the finish line for him. Maybe he just wants to get out and breathe the mountain air. Least, that's how I'm approaching this whole adventure. Maybe I make it, maybe I don't. I'm okay with either so long as I get some fresh air along the way."

❦

Skunkers and Bawdy left the bar, stumbled towards the motor lodge. They carried Coyote draped between them like a wet rag. He'd tried to keep drinking on pace with Skunkers. Which was silly, because he had half the body mass and a tenth the tolerance. It had been funny for a while, but then cycled from silly to obnoxious to straight up annoying, and finally came back around to silly with Coyote slumped over and snoring with his head in a bowl of pretzels.

Back at the motor lodge, the plan was simple. Sneak in all quiet and scout the area, get the lay of the land and see what was what. Maybe Flutterby had already somehow managed to scare Ella off. This plan stalled before it got started. They couldn't turn the key in the lock, kept working at it and whispering until finally Flutterby whipped the door open. She gave them a painfully sharp look before hissing, "Whichever one of you chumps didn't let *her* into our room can sleep in my bed."

The room had two full-sized beds. Flutterby occupied one and Ella the other. Skunkers dumped Coyote on the floor, tucked him partially under a chair. Winked at Bawdy and flumped down into Flutterby's bed. Bawdy grimaced, cast about for open floor space, realized there really wasn't any with the disgorged contents of five packs spread about, grimaced again, and snuck into Ella's bed. Took her about seven seconds to rope an arm around him.

❦

It was a genuine treat to be sleeping in a bed again, even one with sandpapery sheets and a hulking mound of a man taking up more than his fair share. The give of the old mattress was a minor miracle, the wafer-thin pillows an all but forgotten luxury. Before this trip, Flutterby had never had much use for sound machines. Now she came to fully appreciate the droning hum of the air conditioner as it washed away all those minor night noises that were so abundant and bothersome on trail or, for that matter, in a motel room shared by five people. And now, free of the restrictive mummy-cut of her sleeping bag for the first time in what seemed like a particularly long decade, she could pull her knees up right tight to her chest.

Drunk or not, Flutterby wasn't worried about Skunkers causing any problems. She'd already spent enough time around this group of guys to know they were okay. More than. And she wasn't entirely sure that she'd mind if he did come looking for more than a bit of mattress.

She woke some time later, found herself suddenly buried

beneath a suffocating mass. Couldn't draw a full breath to save her life. Took a little doing, but she was able to burrow her way out from under the dead weight that was Skunkers' still-sleeping body. He was clenching his teeth, tossing, turning and otherwise having one of his nightmares. Poor guy did this in the shelter a lot, but since they all assumed it was a symptom of PTSD, a little souvenir he brought back from the war, nobody much complained. Figured that would be like protesting the homecoming troops or something. He hadn't yet woken anyone else, but she sensed he was gathering steam. By the light of her phone, Flutterby could make out the contortions on his face and a soppy wet brow.

She didn't know what else to do, so she started simple. Tried flipping him back over onto his stomach. Reclaim a little mattress room for herself. She couldn't flip him outright, but she could move him back some. He was in mid-moan when she first put hands on him. He quieted down so quickly it was like she'd hit an off-switch. When she took her hands away, the moaning kept on as if it hadn't been interrupted. Seemed even a single fingertip was enough to help calm him.

Using pillows, Flutterby propped herself up against the bed's headboard. Put a cool hand to Skunkers' hot forehead. Watched his jaw go slack.

She sat there in the dark and thought how this was the most use anyone had had for her in bed in far too long. Which inevitably led her to think back on her marriage.

Had spent almost eighteen months married to a doctor. A nice, quiet guy, about as unassuming as doctors come. If he hadn't acted entirely red-blooded and normal during their "courtship" he'd acted close enough to fool her. Problem was, he *was* acting and he *did* fool her. Didn't hardly consummate the wedding and it was all downhill from there. Flutterby's married friends had always talked about the irrevocable diminishing of their sex-lives, but nothing they said had prepared her for a complete cessation of physical contact. Her bridal whites hadn't even been stuffed back in the box yet.

Spent those first six months thinking she was the problem. Was it her body? Her breath? Something else? It drove her mad. Made her feel undesirable, unattractive and maybe a wee bit repulsive. Tried all sorts of crazy ideas: costumes, role play, dirty talk. She acted passive, she acted aggressive. Didn't matter what she did, he wasn't interested. And he wouldn't talk about it beyond assuring her everything was fine and making excuses. He was tired, he was swamped at work, he had a headache.

They spent the next six months working with various marriage counselors. Talked about feelings. Talked about intimacy. Talked about a future together. She came to understand that he genuinely seemed to want the marriage to work, but mostly because he wanted to feel like he was supposed to feel. He wanted to feel how she felt, how most people felt. At the end of that time, one of the counselors pulled her aside, confidentially shared an off-the-record opinion. He wasn't, strictly speaking, entirely comfortable with his sexuality. Best clinical guess, his tendencies leaned towards the asexual.

In retrospect, Flutterby suspected he'd known that he wasn't "normal", but he'd gone ahead and married her with the hopeful intentions of limping through a shared and largely platonic life.

It was all about paperwork during those last six months. Her feelings were hurt terribly, it was a crushing blow to her ego.

Wasn't any malice or ill will on his part. If possible, he was more disappointed than she was about the whole thing. The divorce was amicable, he gave her more than she asked for in the settlement. Was like he was saying, take whatever you want, please, just don't make me touch you.

He bought her out of their house. Instead of relocating locally, continuing to work together in the same hospital, Flutterby quit her job. Moved across the country, came back home to live with her mother. She was a good nurse and there were plenty of hospitals on the east coast. When she was ready, she could get a job in any one of them.

It was early morning when Coyote woke. It took him a bit to process that he was looking up at the dusty underside of a chair. The dingy motel room spun round in his head as he struggled to sit up and then, when the spinning subsided, to stand. There was just enough gray light coming in around the edges of the curtains for him to see Flutterby sitting up in bed, head resting back against the headboard. She was asleep with Skunkers' head pillowed on her thigh.

Then Coyote stumbled a few steps into the bathroom and started to retch.

There was a grassy lot next to the Hot Springs post office. Between errands, many thru-hikers used this space as an outdoor lounge. After picking up his maildrop, Mad Chatter hunkered down and started sifting through the box's contents.

"Got no one at home," he told Bartleby, "had to package these up myself, and ship them out months ago. Been so long now, I can't 'member what's inside. Sorta like Christmas morning. Heh-heh."

Turned out, Chatter gave himself a new pair of hiking socks, toilet paper and AAA lithium ion batteries. Two scoops of pills: various vitamins and assorted doctor prescribed pharmaceuticals. A gallon-sized baggie bulging with homemade jerky. He shared it around—it was spicy hot delicious. A twenty-ounce soda bottle was topped full of a brown liquid Chatter simply called "Blue." Shared a sip of that as well to wash down the jerky. There were also baggies of dried beans and grains and one of Werther's Original Hard Candies.

Next, a white envelope with the message, "Keep on Keeping On to Damascus" written in a loopy scrawl across the outside. A single crisp hundred dollar bill was tucked inside.

Lastly, Chatter removed a smaller box. Placed it there on the grass between them and reverently opened the top. Mad Chatter's face lit up and Bartleby's cringed. His first thought: The old guy sent himself a dead rat. But it wasn't a dead rat, or a live rat or anything else from the Order Rodentia.

It was a coonskin cap. A thick ruff of gray-brown fur with a foot long, black-ringed raccoon tail hanging down off the back.

"Hot damn," Chatter said, beamingly proud of the hat. Set his aviator cap and cracked goggles aside and settled the coonskin cap on his head. "Tell me true—how do I look?"

🍁

Bartleby walked over the French Broad River and out of Hot Springs with eighteen ramen noodle bricks in tow. The noodles, a big no-name jar of peanut butter and a dozen sleeves of orange cardboardy sandwich crackers made up the bulk of his food bag. He'd also found a big baggie of raisins and some yellow drink mix powder in a free hiker box.

All told, the resupply cost him about twelve dollars. Which was about as cheap as he could have reasonably hoped for.

He couldn't afford anything exciting like tuna packets or bagels or even the Dollar General brand mac and cheese. Bartleby never figured he'd arrive at a point in his life where he considered generic mac and cheese too pricey. And surprisingly, that's exactly the point on which he was precariously perched.

Would've been nice to spend the night in town, shower, eat a meal, drink a few beers even, but Bartleby's meager funds were already running low. Much as he could, he intended to preserve them, stretch this whole thing out as far as it would go.

Under the very best circumstances, Lazy JoJo didn't like rodents. This dislike was a life-long sentiment, but basically a passive one. Similar to how one may dislike the thumping of a dryer when the load isn't properly balanced. More often than not, with a little patience, the problem goes away all by itself.

Her dislike became active after a morning in the Smokies when she'd discovered a crew of rodent robbers had chewed a hole into the top pocket of her pack. Annoyingly enough, the pocket hadn't been zipped closed, was in fact flapping wide open not two inches above the new mouse hole. There was absolutely no need for the little buggers to gnaw themselves a private entrance. And if that forced entry wasn't bad enough, the mice promptly sniffed out and tracked down the baggie of Cheez-Its she'd forgotten in there. They helped themselves to a right jolly feast of unnatural cheesy goodness. Ate or absconded with maybe a quarter of the crackers. Defecated on the remaining three-quarters.

It was this last act, the befouling of the food they didn't eat, that pushed JoJo over the line to actively disliking mice.

And being the kind of woman who likes to set out and solve her own problems, the first purchase JoJo made in Hot Springs was a six-pack of cheap wooden mouse traps.

First night back on trail, Spring Mountain Shelter was mostly full. That didn't stop her from laying the traps out with strategic cunning and little dabs of peanut butter for bait.

Got her first mouse before the sun went down.

❦ ❦ ❦

"Gumdrops."

"Jelly beans."

"Hershey kisses."

"Diamonds."

Skunkers had his shoes off, was slipping into a pair of dry socks or "freshies" as he liked to call them. Flutterby sat nearby, reading from the register.

"What're they going on about now?" he asked her.

"V.A. Moose wrote something in here asking what unicorn

poop might look like."

"Gold nuggets," Coyote said.

Skunkers gave Flutterby a confused look. She could only shake her head.

"Or," Bawdy was thinking hard about this unicorn question, "or maybe flowers. Yeah, that's it. I bet unicorns poop little blooming flowers out. Hey—" this directed to Skunkers, "—you about done here? We haven't seen a drop of water all day, I still don't understand how your socks are soaked."

"Of course his socks are wet," Coyote said. "Big Boy's got the sweatiest feet going. Soaks right through his shoes."

❧ ❧ ❧

Register: Little Laurel Shelter

4/29 Hiking strong and walk-
       ing long. Appalachian woods
       are where I belong.

                          High-Ku

❧ ❧ ❧

Bartleby took lunch by himself at Little Laurel Shelter.

A big guy came thumping along trail heading south. He'd already started talking before he got within fifteen yards of the table, "You're thru-hiking, right? I thru-hiked in '06. Awesome time. Summited Katahdin in a snowstorm. Couldn't barely get a picture of the sign up there."

The guy had a braided pony-tail and shoulders almost as

wide as Blitz. Was wearing a too-tight tank top half-shirt and a hiking skirt which, to be fair, could've been one of those unisex hiking kilts. It was hard to make the same case for the stripper-red lipstick or the eye shadow. Also, the guy had no thumbs. Bartleby didn't immediately register the missing digits, but it came as a small shock when he did.

"Name's Diesel Donna," he said. "I got king-size Snickers for thru-hikers. You want?"

"Yeah, sure. Thanks."

Bartleby first noticed the missing thumbs during the candy bar hand-off. He had to clamp down his initial instinct to drop the Snickers like it was hot.

"I just heard about a dude going by K2. You meet him yet?"

Bartleby shook his head.

"Guess he got his gear at K-Mart. Pack, boots, tent—absolutely everything down to the Coghlan's combination compass/emergency whistle. Says he's hiking from K-Mart to Katahdin. Hence the name K2." Donna snorted, shook his head, "You really do get all kinds out here, huh?"

In the following days, Bartleby spent long miles wondering how Diesel Donna ever flagged down a hitch back in '06.

Flutterby was still shaken up when she got to Jerry's Cabin Shelter. She'd taken a real doozy, a boots over backpack tumble along the fine-toothed white-rock ridgeline leading down from Big Firescald Knob. Misstepped, lost her balance and went down hard. Scraped skin from her knee, her shin and an elbow in the process. None of which required stitches, but each still throbbed and oozed blood when the shelter's low roof came into view.

Jerry's Cabin was squat and ugly with a back-canted floor that was particularly uninviting.

"Looks like a big ol' mouse house," Skunkers volunteered.

"A real rodentorium," Bawdy agreed. They watched Flutterby limp into camp.

"Happened to you, Flubs?"

"That last downhill was not very nice to me."

Coyote grinned, "I know, it sucked right? Up and down, up and down, up and down on all those slick-sharp white rocks. I was like to fall over."

"Well, I did fall over," Flutterby snapped. She dropped her pack, took out a bandana, used it to dab at her bloody scrapes.

"That looks bad."

"It feels worse. What time is it?"

"Sixteen forty-seven."

Flutterby gave Skunkers a healthy scowl, "I think it's weird that such a fancy watch can't tell normal time."

"Oh, it can, but see, I got it set to military—"

"So either translate it to civilian time or simply sit there quietly like a big dope when I ask for the time, okay? We'll all pretend you don't have a four pound watch sitting on your wrist. That military time is absolutely crap and worse than nothing at all."

"It's four forty-seven," Skunkers mumbled.

❧

It was shaping up to be a real grungry night in camp. Everybody was grumpy and hungry and otherwise out of sorts.

"Hey Bawds, hook a brotha up with some denatured alcohol. I forgot to refill back in Hot Springs."

"How terribly convenient," Bawdy groused as he passed his fuel bottle over.

"Come on now—you don't think I wouldn't fill up so I could save weight and leech off your goodwill?"

This was exactly what Bawdy suspected, but he didn't bother saying so.

Walking from his tent to the table, Skunkers stubbed his toe. Hopped around yelping like an idiot.

"Why you always going around barefoot?" Coyote wanted to know. "It's like you're a little kid or a hobbit with those filthy feet."

"Gotta let the dogs dry, dude. Don't wanna get trench foot or nuttin'."

Tetchy as Bawdy was, this was the last straw. "Say nothing," he said to Skunkers.

"Nuttin'."

"Nothing. No-THING."

"Nuttin'."

"No-THING. Some-THING."

"Suttin'."

"There's an I-N-G right there at the end. Don't you hear it?"

"Fucked if that's not what I'm sayin'. Nuttin'."

"Sounds like you're going out to pick nuts off a nut tree. I mean, I know you're a country mouse an all, Skunks, but I'm starting to wonder what country exactly."

❧

"Told you not to do that near me," Skunkers growled.

Finished with his dinner, Coyote had his mouth wide open, was working at his teeth with a length of floss. Every so often he spit a mouthful of bloody saliva into the firepit.

"Uuummumumka," Coyote retorted with his hands still deep in his mouth. His words weren't exactly clear, but their meaning was: go pound sand.

Skunkers shrugged once, as if things had escalated up and out of his control. Then he leaned to the side and loosed a rolling thunderclap of a fart, the first in a series of noxious explosions that quickly and thoroughly fouled the surrounding area.

Bawdy and Flutterby scurried out of the area of effect, with little harm done. But, of course, they weren't the intended target. Coyote, with his gag-reflex and delicate constitution, wasn't so lucky. Got one whiff and started up choking. Went down on one knee, gagging with tears in his eyes.

"Welcome to Stink Central," Bawdy heckled. "Population: you."

There was a random little mushroom cluster of gravestones in a clearing just north of Big Butt Mountain. No more than a foot off trail. Two of them had the look of old stone tablets; over the decades, wind and weather had made their markings mostly illegible. These flanked a newer stone dedicated to one Milliard

F. Haire. Milliard had died July 1, 1863 at the age of thirteen.

Pony unbuckled his hipbelt and let his pack slip to the ground, "Good a place as any for a break, right?"

Bartleby didn't think so, but his legs were tired and it was another three or four miles still to Flint Mountain Shelter and the end of another hiking day. Pony started on a handful of Slim Jims while Bartleby worked through a big bag of raisins. Only three days out of Hot Springs and already he'd come to understand why someone might leave raisins behind in a hiker box. They looked like dried up rabbit turds and they went down like bits of old leather.

Didn't mean to, didn't want to, but Bartleby snuck a peak over at the grave markers. In recent weeks, someone had placed a bunch of fresh flowers between them. Most of the petals had turned brown and fallen away.

He'd been chugging along at a decent pace, minding his business and thinking nothing much at all. The unexpected sight of these gravestones started Bartleby's mind thinking about his own father.

On the whole, these thoughts were unwelcome.

When Bartleby's father died, his body had been cremated, but in the years since, the family hadn't gotten around to burying him. There was always some reason to put it off. As far as Bartleby knew, the heavy marble urn still sat collecting dust on a bookshelf in the room that had served as the office for the family business.

During the worst of the bad time, when the business was being sucked under by an unfortunate confluence of events, Bartleby hated walking into that office. Seeing the urn and knowing he'd somehow ruined everything his father had worked for. He'd tried moving it, hiding it behind accounting binders, but his mother had a weird radar for the urn. Always returned it to its proper place. Got so some days, Bartleby couldn't even make himself go into the office.

Even now, separated by a distance of a few years and fifteen hundred miles, thinking about the office and the business and the banks and creditors who kept the phone ringing all day long made Bartleby's stomach clench like a fist.

"Only thirteen, huh?" Pony said. "Wonder how they died."

Bartleby opened his eyes, "Huh?"

Pony pointed at the central stone, "And what kind of name is Milliard, anyway?"

A boy's name, Bartleby guessed, but before he could say so Mad Chatter and Sweet Jane the Greatest Dane wandered up trail.

When Chatter let go her leash, Jane barreled straight for Pony and his Slim Jims. The postman froze. A high-pitched squeal slipped from the back of his throat. Luckily for him, Bartleby caught Jane up as she went by. Pulled her in tight, wrestled her around and started scratching behind her ears. It wasn't long before she settled down, Pony and his pseudo-meat sticks at least temporarily forgotten.

"Been meaning to ask," Pony called to Chatter, "what's with the getup?"

"Getup?"

"That fur hat. Gotta be hot as hell."

"This is a genuine coonskin cap, son. My personal nod to the king of the wild frontier, Tennessee's own folk hero, frontiersman and congressional representative—Davy Crockett."

"Okay, I get that. But what about before, with the hat and

goggles?"

"First flight."

This didn't make things any clearer for Pony.

"The Wright Brothers," Bartleby clarified, "North Carolina."

"Very good, Bumblebee," Chatter said. He lobbed a small, gold-foil wrapped candy at Bartleby. Hit him in the arm. It tasted a whole lot better than old raisins.

"What's that? Werther's Original? My Na-Na used to keep a dish of them on the mantle," Pony said. Hope glinted in his soft brown eyes, "They're made with *fresh* butter and *real* cream."

"That they are," Chatter tossed a candy to Pony and winked. He gave the headstones a quick glance, "What do you think, Jane? This a decent spot?"

Jane didn't look over. She was too busy sniffing the bottom of Bartleby's shoes.

"Yeppers, I think so too." Chatter began rummaging around in the depths of his pack. "Bumblebee, Pony, would you gentlemen join me in a toast?"

Once he located it, Chatter opened the ziploc, took a pinch of something between his fingers and dribbled it over the graves.

Pony's eyes widened, "Are those ashes?"

Chatter tucked the baggy away, took a sip of whiskey and passed the bottle around.

"My late wife, Jane. Gone these two years now."

"Oh, I'm so sorry—" Pony began.

"Yes," Chatter shook his head sadly, "she was a real...castrating clam. I been wanting to get out here and hike the AT for twenty-five years. My wife, I call her Bitter Jane, wouldn't let me go. She hated the outdoors, she hated me—the woman hated everything. It was touch and go for a while there, but I guess I finally waited her out." His eyes sparkled, "She always wanted to be buried on her family's plot back in Wisconsin."

❦ ❦ ❦

Something heavy spronged against the tent fly. A fat-ass toad maybe. Whatever it was, the point of impact was near enough to Tortoise's head to wake her from a fitful sleep.

Mostly, her sleep had been fitful because the sleeping Hair-brained had somehow driven her off her sleeping pad and up against the wall of the tent. Also, he was sawing wood on pace to match a mid-sized lumber mill.

"Move over," she whispered. No response. She followed up with a sharp elbow.

Not only did this fail to wake Hairbrained, it somehow failed to even momentarily disrupt his snoring. It took another few elbows, an ear flick and, finally, a ruthless tug of facial hair to bring him mostly awake.

"Whazz happin'?"

"What's happening is you're on *my* side of the tent; you got me pushed half-off *my* sleeping pad and you're pinning *my* sleeping bag. I can't sleep."

"I'm bigger," he explained. Then, "Wanna have sex?"

"No. I want you to move over; I want you to stop pinning me."

Hairbrained was asleep and snoring again before Tortoise finished talking.

In frustration, she drove her shoulder against his body, tried to roll him over, tried to move him out of her sleeping space. He gave no indication of impending accommodation.

Growling low in her throat, and with an arm crooked over like a chicken wing, Tortoise rained a wild storm of pointed-elbow flipper attacks down upon the snoring Hairbrained.

This was not close to anything he could even pretend to sleep through.

"What the hell?!"

As her elbow continued to rise and fall with a frenzied vigor, she snarl-shrieked, "Stop pinning, stop pinning, stop pinning! Move over, move over, move over!"

"Jesus, I'm over, okay?" he said after evacuating the contested ground. "You *really* gotta learn how to share."

"I still don't recognize you," Bawdy said when he came up on Coyote. He was sprawled amidst some fresh young curls of fern and stuffing whole Twinkies into his mouth. They could see clear down to Sams Gap where little blurs of movement were inching along US-23. Bawdy dropped his pack and sat down on it.

"I know, huh?" Coyote nodded. "New pack, new shoes, new clothes. Even got me some new headwear."

He was referring to the danbanna he'd picked up in Hot Springs. It had a bandana-like paisley print but was specifically tailored to wear on one's head. Made him look more ridiculous than usual, like the pirate character from the Village People (if they had a pirate).

Instead of pointing this out, Bawdy poured a packet of Cherry Kool-Aid into a water bottle. Gave it a hearty shake and took a long chug.

He stopped drinking only to let a mighty belch erupt from his inner depths.

"That stuff good?"

"Oh, yyyyeeeeaaaahhhh," Bawdy said in his best impersonation of the Kool-Aid Guy.

"You got yourself some big red clown lips."

"Don't care. And anyway, with your new getup, you're looking pretty weird too. Like when someone first gets contacts and stops wearing glasses and their face looks totally off."

Coyote shrugged and continued licking at a Twinkie wrapper.

"Everything fit? Working better?"

He grunted, "Not really. New shoes come complete with new blisters, I guess. The pack's like half a pound lighter, but it's got no padding in the shoulder straps, so they're cutting ruts into my shoulders. All told, I did manage to shave off twelve, maybe thirteen ounces. "

"What'd that cost ya?"

"Hey, it's like the man said, 'Simplify, simplify, simplify'."

"That's not exactly what Thoreau meant—"

"How about, 'Less is more'. Does that one work?"

"Not really. You went the 'more is less' route."

"Okay, then, let's chalk it up to retail therapy. Nearly broke my heart to see Skunkers' head resting in Flubby's lap."

"Might've been you, if you hadn't gotten so sloppy drunk."

"Nah. For all my sniffing around, I never had a sniff."

"Think something's going on with them now?"

"Dunno. What's going on with you and Frecklebutt?"

"Ginger Nut? Nothing—why?"

"You two looked pretty chummy back at the motor lodge."

"No way, hombre."

"Well, someone's gotta step up. That girl needs a good wooden spoon across the ass."

"When you say stuff like that, it makes me wonder who you really are."

"Yeah? And who are you?"

"I'm definitely not the man for *that* job." Pause. "Hey, am I being a baby or has the temperature dropped?"

"Well, you're probably being a baby, but it does feel chillier."

"Sorta looks like snow too, doesn't it?"

"It doesn't snow in Tennessee, you donk."

"Didn't say it was gonna snow, just that it looked like it."

❦

Register: Hogback Ridge Shelter

4/31 Snowed on us last night. In Tennessee. One day shy of May. WTF?!? It's officially colder than penguin poop.   - SQUIRTzzzz

4/31 Colder than a meat locker. Mmmmm...meat...
                                      Skunkers

4/31 Colder than it was before I bounced my insulated jacket up to Maine.   Coyote Slick

4/31 Colder than a brass bra.   Flutterby

4/31 Colder than an arctic ass-fuck.   —Bawdy-Boy

4/31 Could be worse...   Green Mountain Man

Newly leafed trees sagged and branches snapped under the unwelcome weight of rime ice. A thin blanket of hoarfrost lay over everything. They spent the morning crunching over snow. Probably less than an inch, but still enough to soak shoes and freeze toes. The trail angled up towards Big Stamp Bald. The higher it took them, the stronger the spiteful wind. Seemed like, no matter how fast or hard or which direction they hiked, it kept catching them head on. Coyote pulled his rain jacket on. Helped to stop some of the icy chill. Skunkers wrapped his head and neck with a desert colored scarf-type *shemagh* he'd taken to wearing over in Iraq.

Cold as it was, they were all still sweating and steaming from the effort. Bawdy resisted the temptation to pull more clothes on. He knew anything he wore now would soak through with sweat, be soppy wet and useless later when he was done hiking and *really* needing warmth. So he kept chugging along with too much exposed skin, chattering teeth and visible breath.

"You hear Ella saying she got shin splints?"

"Yeah," Coyote said. "Think she'll go off trail?"

"We should be so lucky."

Coyote grunted, "What are they exactly?"

"Dunno. Everything I know about shin splints, I learned from *The Old Man and the Sea*," Bawdy said.

"What's that?" Skunkers asked.

"That Joe DiMaggio had 'em."

"No, what's that other thing? The old man thing?"

"It's a book, Skunks. A classic by Ernest Hemmingway. You really gotta expand your horizons."

"I'm going to college."

"Yeah?"

"Yeah. Why you think I went into the army? G.I. Bill's gonna pay my way."

"They still do that? What a racket."

"Survive one week over in Iraq and then tell me it's a racket, Slick."

Bawdy asked, "What school is gonna let your goofy ass in?"

"Southern Suwannee College. Already applied and everything."

"Never heard of it."

"Shows how much you know Professor Fraudy—it's Ivy League."

"Are you joking? No it isn't."

"Yeah it is. Ivy League of the South. Said so right on their web page."

"That's not real Ivy League. That's like saying Frosh football is the same as the NFL."

When skunkers looked to Coyote for support, Coyote shook his head, "Sorry, man."

After a full month of hiking, most thru-hikers got so they would eat just about anything put in front of them, but they all still had go-to favorites.

Flutterby packed a few apples and maybe some green spinach or an onion to spruce up the first few dinners out. Most mornings she mixed instant coffee, hot cocoa and oatmeal packets together to make a lumpy hot breakfast drink with some kick.

Must've been a billy goat somewhere back in Skunkers' family tree. There really wasn't much of anything he wouldn't eat. Grew up on Knorr dinners, McDoubles and day-glow orange mac and cheese. Which is exactly what he ate on trail. The more processing and sawdust that went into a food product, the more he liked it. The hotter the better too. A couple splashes of Tabasco sauce, enough crushed red pepper and he might've been convinced to eat a cold bowl of mud.

Coyote's food choices were based less on taste than caloric capacity. He wanted lots of oomph per ounce, and so leaned towards squeeze bottles of liquid margarine, tubs of peanut butter and handfuls of almonds and walnuts. He'd heard good things about lard and would've tried it if he could've figured how to get his hands on some.

Lazy JoJo packed dehydrated milk and carnation instant breakfast powder. Had herself a strawberry shake most evenings after the day's hike.

When it worked out, Old Man Trouble bought and boiled himself a dozen eggs in town. Ate them as he walked trail. Kept dinner (a homemade whole grain pilaf mix) interesting with sun-dried tomatoes, cloves of garlic and lots of olive oil.

Every time she returned to the woods, Two-Speed Tortoise carried baby peeled carrots and an avocado or two. She learned to love the chocolaty richness of Nutella spread on bagels, pita bread and crackers. In the tent, after Hairbrained fell asleep, she sometimes nibbled clandestine bars of dark chocolate.

Whenever he could find them, Pony Express went in for yogurt dipped snacks. Pretzels, almonds, raisins, goji berries—it didn't much matter so long as they were smothered in yogurt.

His favorite lunch became cream cheese, cashew butter and honey smeared on tortillas.

Mad Chatter gravitated towards quinoa, fancy cheese and hard salami. Wild ramps too, when they were in season. Jane pretty much ate anything, but she seemed to have a soft spot for butterflies.

Generally, Bawdy put a hurting on a six-pack of Little Debbie Swiss Cake Rolls as soon as he hit town. For the first time in his life he could indulge his weakness for junk food with a guiltless abandon. For dinner he regularly enjoyed cheese tortellinis smothered under drifts of grated parmesan and garlic powder.

Bartleby didn't have the luxury of eating what he liked. Mostly he made do with random selections from hiker boxes—noodles, plain old peanuts, cup-a-soups and the like. It wasn't exciting, but sometimes it was illuminating. Turned out that he liked ginger tea, prunes and banana chips far more than he ever would've guessed.

Skunkers' bladder was about to burst. He'd been putting off peeing for a couple of hours, but enough was enough already. Climbing out of his tent, he was surprised to see snatches of light and motion showing through Bawdy's tarp.

After watering the bushes, Skunkers went over. "What're you doing, Bawds?"

When Bawdy didn't answer, Skunkers squatted down, peeked under the tarp flap.

Bawdy was sound asleep with a book lying open on his chest. He'd left his headlamp on. A flickering flock of moths, three or four dozen, lined the tarp's inner wall, tiptoed the length of Bawdy's forearms and fluttered around his face.

Skunkers reached in, all quiet and careful, and toggled the light off.

✿ ✿ ✿

Somehow, even after the snow melted, the seasonal spring was all but dry. Barely a puddle really. It was far too shallow to pump from or even to properly scoop from. But it was the only water source for a mile or two in any direction, so they were trying to make do.

Towards that end, Lazy JoJo held a bottle while Pony used its cap to ladle an ounce at a time. After eight or ten capfuls, they had to stop and wait for the water level to rise again. Since any water they did wrangle was chock full of swirling sediment, Bartleby then poured it through an ad-hoc filter (dirty bandana folded over on itself) before adding purification drops.

In thirty minutes, they'd managed to procure almost three quarts of brownish water. Between the three of them, they needed twice that amount to get through the night.

"Be easier to hike ahead. Book says there's water in a mile or so," Pony said.

"Feel free, but I gotta stay here," Bartleby said, "no tent."

JoJo grunted noncommittally.

Pony sighed, "Guess if I cook a Mountain House, I can probably survive on a quart and a half."

"Seriously? You're carrying freeze dried food?" Poohbah snorted.

"Low sodium Chicken Alfredo. My—"

"Those meals cost way too much, they taste like congealed plastic and even after choking it down, you still gotta carry all that packaging out."

Pony's ears turned red. He straightened up, jabbed his screw cap/ladle in Poohbah's direction, "As I was going to say before you cut me off, the Mountain House dinner was part of a going away present from my sister. But since it doesn't meet your exacting standards, I guess I should just throw it away and eat nothing tonight. For once in your miserable little life, would that actually make you happy? I'll do it if you think there's even a sliver of a chance of it somehow actually making you happy."

Poohbah didn't have any retort ready to fire back, so Pony kept going. "All your negativity, it's like a...a....a used condom. I mean, it's just yucky. Take it off already."

The AT zigzagged sharp as new saw teeth in the last half mile down into Erwin, Tennessee. The trail squirted across the Nolichucky River and some parallel running train tracks before disappearing again into the woods. Maybe a grand total of point-two miles of trail overlapped actual paved road.

But before the AT returned back to the woods, it passed by a hiker hostel. At one point in the distant past, the place must've been a simple, single story residence. Over time, the pell-mell addition of decks and fences, stone walkways, bunkrooms, private cabins, bathhouses and picnic tables had helped complete the transformation from non-descript home to cluttered and unkempt clusterfuck. There was a stinking full dumpster of garbage right out front, partially hidden behind a row of soda machines. Except for a lack of seagulls wheeling overhead, the place vaguely reminded Two-Speed Tortoise of a town dump.

Didn't much matter though. She was out of food and foot-sore and ready to come in out of the cold that was both unreasonable and unseasonable. Sleepy-eyed hikers were milling around, loafing at the picnic tables. Didn't see him, but she knew Hairbrained must be around somewhere. She'd barely gotten her pack off when an old man appeared at her elbow.

"Welcome and good morning, sweetheart," he said.

"Thanks," Tortoise said, "happy to be here."

"Looks like maybe you could appreciate a hot cup of coffee on this cold morning."

"That sounds really good."

"Cream, sugar?"

"Please."

The man ducked inside, came out carrying a steaming mug. Handed it over, watched her take her first sip.

"Thanks. Hmmmm. Haven't had coffee since Hiawassee."

"Good right?

"Uh-huh, it sure is."

He smiled crookedly, "That'll be two dollars."

❦

When she found him, Hairbrained had already picked up their maildrops. He was elbow deep in the various supplies and foodstuffs.

"Think you got something from Callie."

Before setting off, Tortoise had put together a list of P.O. addresses with expected arrival dates. Posted this list on Facebook, encouraging any and all care packages that friend or family might see fit to send.

Against the wishes of her closet allies, Tortoise had gone ahead and taken a semester off from school to follow Hairbrained out onto trail. They'd been dating on and off, mostly on during drunken weekend nights and off during holidays and school breaks. Her parents thought he was pond scum. Her best friend, Callie, knew he was.

Pond scum or no, Hairbrained was a year older, had just graduated after nine semesters, and when he cared to, he could make Tortoise feel great. Initially, he'd planned to disappear on this grand adventure with a college buddy and leave Tortoise high and dry for five months, if he even came back to her at all. When his buddy accepted an unexpected job offer, it didn't take long for Hairbrained to talk Tortoise into joining him. Sure, he painted her an overly romantic and otherwise unrealistic picture of the hike. And of his feelings for her. More than that though, she'd never really done much of anything exciting or out of the ordinary. Seemed like an opportunity she might regret if she let it slip away.

Callie sent Tortoise a gossipy note, a hollow chocolate bunny, three Cadbury crème eggs, a sack of assorted Starburst Jelly Beans, twelve ounces of pastel colored M&M's and a big puffy roll of toilet paper. This food was wrapped protectively in what turned out to be a pair of eggshell blue running shorts. They sported two yellow athletic stripes racing down each side. In the note, Callie had written, "Don't know why, but these 'Fancy Pants' reminded me of you.

＊　＊　＊

Just north of Erwin, Tennessee, the AT crossed two sets of train tracks. It was easy to tell that the tracks were active because of the train idling there on them. From where Pony Express stood, down off the raised rail bed, train cars stretched off as far as he could see in either direction. The entire line of cars trembled and hummed with a tangible impatience. Linkages chunked and steel wheels squealed forward an inch at a time. Less frequently, a distant engine whistle would bleat out warnings.

Clearly, things were about to happen.

＊

Bartleby looked left, looked right and shrugged, "Been here long?"

"Fifteen, maybe twenty minutes." Pony sat on his pack with his journal on his lap. "Should go any time now. Find any Aquamira?"

"Uh-uh. Rumor is it's all been rerouted to Japan. With the tsunami and everything, I guess they need it more than I do."

"That sucks."

"I scored some bleach back at the hostel. A drop or two should kill most anything swimming in my water."

"Seriously?" The postman winced, "That can't be good for you."

"Least of my worries."

Just then the train jerked ahead a yard or more.

Pony jumped up, eager as a schoolboy for recess, "And here we go."

❦

Lazy JoJo slowed down long enough to shift the toothpick from one side of her mouth to the other, "One a you hurt or sumpin'?"

Blitz was sprawled on his sleeping pad, dozing. Bartleby had his shoes off, was working his thumbs into the tender meat around his heel. Finished with his journal, Pony Express was recounting his first sighting of a wild California Condor. Old Man Trouble was shelling a hard-boiled egg and pretending to listen.

"No, no," Pony Express said. "Just waiting for this stupid train to roll out of here." He would've gone on longer, but it was obvious JoJo wasn't listening. She pulled herself up the ladder rungs of the nearest railcar. Even with her pack on, she squeezed through the space between cars, disappeared down the far side and kept right on hiking.

❦ ❦ ❦

It wasn't any kind of surprise that Ella was the first to hear the news. If she wasn't walking or sleeping and could get any kind of cell signal, that smartphone of hers was powered up and keeping tabs on the wide world.

"Says they got bin Laden," she said. There was an excited tremble in her voice, like maybe she'd played a pivotal part in breaking the story of the year.

Coyote was schooling Skunkers in cribbage. This news caught him mid-peg and actually stopped him cold, "Who got him? How'd he die?"

Skunkers banged a fist on the table, "Fucking righteous!"

"Seriously, Frecklebutt, how'd he die?"

"I don't know. Says American special forces raided a compound in Pakistan on intel that Osama bin Laden had been hiding there. He was killed during a gunfight. It happened last night, I guess."

"Yeah, but how? They shoot him? Blow him up? Hang him high?"

"Booya! Boo and Ya, baby! Who cares, Yote? That dude has been on deck for a beat down since '01 and we finally served him up." Skunkers high-fived Shaggy Bob, Ella and anyone else in reach.

"That's fine and all, but seriously...how you think he died, Skunks? Shot down? Blown up? Knifed? Poisoned?"

"How do I know?"

"I don't know, weren't you some kind of Green Beret or something?"

"Ranger, dude."

"So—gimme your best guess."

Skunkers leaned back, took a moment to think it through, "I don't know nuttin' from nuttin', but if we put boots on the ground at some fortified compound, I doubt we blew him up. I mean, anything can happen in a firefight, grenades or hand-to-hand combat, but I'm guessing Osama took one in the head."

"Goddamn," Coyote groaned.

"S'all good, Yote. Dead is dead and Osama be dead."

"I was in a pool. Couple of guys on my block, we each put up five grand. Everyone agreed that bin Laden wasn't long for this life, but we couldn't agree on how he'd go. I had him getting blown up. Figured we'd drop a Tomahawk or, I don't know, nuke the whole Middle East or something."

❦

Register: No Business Knob Shelter

5/2 Obama v. Osama
     It took a few rounds but finally Osama got
     Obama'd!!!   Shaggy Bob

5/2 Wouldn't have minded pulling that trigger.
                              Sgt. Skunkers

5/2 Glad to see him go, but why risk American lives when
     we coulda carpet-bombed the Abbotabad compound
     instead?   Coyote

5/2 How is killing Osama any different or better than
     what he's done? Ain't murder, murder? Just askin'.
     —BawdyBoy@DevilsAdvocate.com

5/2 Does this mean we can bring our people home and
     start fixing the economy, the polarized political
     system and/or global warming? Just askin'.
                         -Flubby Pie

Heat three cups water in an oversized titanium cook pot. Bring to a roiling boil, unless low on stove fuel or patience, in which case, warmish water will suffice. Be sure to remove all bugs and floating debris.

Add two bricks of ramen noodles with accompanying oriental flavor packets. Simmer until noodles are soft(ish). Add one envelope (4.1oz) potato flakes. Idahoan: Baby Reds— Roasted Garlic & Parmesan flavor recommended, but any will serve. Stir thoroughly, making sure excess water is absorbed and all potato flakes have fully congealed to their intended paste-like consistency. Add one (2.6oz) envelope of Starkist: Chunk Light Tuna in sunflower oil. If available, the (4.5oz) envelope of Starkist: Tuna Creations—Sweet & Spicy adds both bulk and zing. One spoonful Butter Buds Sprinkles: Butter Flavor Granules. Two mini-bottles, Tabasco brand hot sauce, lovingly saved from MRE rations and returned stateside upon completion of tour of duty in Iraq. Three heaping spoonfuls of additional grated parmesan cheese, if any survived the previous night's dinner. Two packets soy sauce (smuggled out of the Gatlinburg Chinese buffet). Also, add as many chunks of cheddar cheese as can be reasonably afforded while reserving enough for tomorrow's lunch. If available, random hunks of pepperoni, cracker crumbs, fresh garlic cloves or sardines would make delightful additions. Borrow Bawdy's garlic powder. A dash or two is plenty unless he isn't paying attention, in which case, treat less like a spice and more like a topping.

Salt and pepper to taste.

If possible, cover and let sit for five minutes. This will allow the cheddar to melt and the dish's distinctive flavors to blend. If waiting is not possible, or after the five minutes have passed, spork it all into your pie-hole as fast as possible without spilling a single drop. Be sure to scrape every morsel of cheesy, noodley-mashed goodness from the pot. Use finger if necessary. Thoroughly lick both spoon and finger clean. Check beard for possible holdouts.

Repeat until full.

❦ ❦ ❦

Curley Maple Gap Shelter. A few miles north of Erwin, TN.

"Somebody please tell me again why we didn't stay in town," Coyote whined.

"I didn't feel like stopping," Flutterby said. "Told you, you should stay if you wanted."

Skunkers sniffed at his pack straps, "Bawdy, smell this, will ya?"

"Yep, that stinks, Skunks."

"Bad, right?"

"I'd say somewhere between super-vile body odor and rotting flesh."

"Yep, that's about what I was thinking."

"I really need a night off trail," Coyote said.

"It's only four miles back to Erwin. Why don't you stop your whining and go get yourself a hotel room or a hooker or whatever it is you're missing so badly," Flutterby suggested.

"Bump that. There isn't a hotel, or a hooker for that matter, in this world, that I'd hike four and a half miles south for. I'm crazy but I'm not *crazy*."

"So shut up, eat your Pop Tarts, drink some water and get your mind around camping up on Beauty Spot in another few miles."

"I'm cold."

"You're getting to be as bad as Bawdy with all your complaining. Why can't the two of you at least pretend to be more like Skunkers?" Because of a trio of hot, new blisters on her foot, Flutterby's tolerance for lame-assery was lower than normal.

"How I'd get brought into this?" Bawdy yelped.

"What," Coyote yapped, "you want *more* Midwestern meatheads in your life?"

Skunkers flexed a melon-sized bicep, "Think she meant a tough guy, Slick."

"I meant contentedly quiet, but okay, 'tough guy' probably works too."

They were still going at it pretty good when Old Man Trouble wandered along. He shook his head at all the racket, "If y'all are ready to hike, I'll tell ya about the first time the trail ever saved my life."

Flutterby was up and wearing her pack in no time. Set off hiking in Trouble's wake and left the boys scurrying to catch up.

"See," Trouble began, "Back in '91, it was a whole different scene on the AT. This was before hiking gear went high-tech and lightweight. Everybody wore heavy leather hiking boots and carried packs plumped full of marginally effective gear.

"I was just a few days out of Damascus. BawdyBoy@Spent the night up in Grayson Highlands. Found this lonely little spot looking down on a pack of wild ponies. There was this beautiful ruby sunset. Went to sleep feeling good about the world, you know? And then it started to rain. Big time. Barrels and barrels of water. First serious rain I'd tented in, and it turned out my hundred and thirty-nine dollar tent wasn't up to the challenge. Thing leaked like a colander. Come morning, I was cold and wet and everything I owned was pretty much sponged up to twice it's normal weight.

"I packed up in the rain. Ate breakfast in the rain. Crapped in the rain. It was miserable. Had to pour a few inches of water out of my boots before pulling them on. The rain kept on all day long. It wasn't freezing out, probably like sixty degrees, but every time I stopped for a break I started up shivering. Had to hurry, get back hiking or I was gonna get hypothermic. This was one of those terrible weather days when nobody who had any choice was out on trail. I was all alone—didn't see another soul.

"Planned on staying the night at Hurricane Mountain Shelter, but when I got there, I couldn't warm up. Shivering like a wet Chihuahua. Nobody there, no way to start a fire, no options but to keep hiking.

"So I set off trudging towards Trimpi Shelter. It was like nine or ten miles further along, which was gonna make it a twenty-five mile day for me without any real rest stops or breaks. Somewhere in those last miles, I started to realize that this silly old man had gotten himself into a spot of trouble. I mean, when I finally got to Trimpi, what was going be different, right? I still didn't have any dry clothes to put on and I was still shivering up a storm. The only difference would be I'd be too tired and hungry to hike to the next shelter.

"When I finally got there Trimpi was something like point-three down a side trail and I stood on the AT trying to decide if I should go down to the shelter or just keep on hiking. Which, I know, isn't any kind of good logic. I swear, I stood there for five minutes, numbly trying to decide what to do before finally slinking down to the shelter. And you know what tipped the scales? I was hoping that it would have a tarp stretched across its opening, you know, like some shelters have. Figured if it did, I'd be able to cut it down, roll up in it and *maybe* survive the night.

"Course when I got down to the shelter, there wasn't anybody there. No tarp neither. I was so disappointed it took a few minutes to register that the shelter had a built in stone fireplace. And some angel had actually left a big ol' pile of kindling wood stacked next to it. It's maybe even odds that I could've survived the night without a fire, but no way would it have been any kind of comfortable."

Just before the climb up to Roan Mountain started for real.

A plastic baggy hung from a branch by a bit of string just before the climb up Roan Mountain got serious. Tucked inside were crude directions to a hostel just half a mile down an unlikely little side trail.

Coyote stopped and waited. When Bawdy and Flutterby appeared he started in, "Since we didn't spend a night in Erwin, I wanna walk down, check this place out. Could use a hot shower and some real food."

"Where's Skunkers?" Flutterby asked.

"Dunno. Never caught him. Ahead, I guess."

"I'm gonna keep on, get this next climb behind me," she said. "We got Damascus coming up in four or five days. I can hold off until then. Besides, it's noonish on a Saturday. Might be some trail magic up at Carvers Gap."

"No chance. We're pretty much cursed trail magic-wise."

She shrugged and started up hiking again. Wanted to ensure that inertia's heavy hand didn't get a good grip on her. "Well," Flutterby called, "I guess if you're lucky, maybe I'll see you two pussyfoots up trail a ways."

Bawdy watched her go. Until half a minute ago, he'd been fully committed to spending the night at Overmountain Shelter. Now the lure of pizza and whatever else this hostel of Coyote's had to offer was sapping his willpower.

"I don't know, Yote. Still got some miles left in these legs."

"What? You're gonna leave me all alone? We been hiking together since Neels Gap."

"I know, but it's so early. We'll make Overmountain easy."

"Listen, I need a shower, I need hot food, I need a soft bed, or a bunk or whatever it is they're offering. You come with, the night's on me. All the pizza or ice cream or beer we can get our hands—my treat."

"Seriously?"

"Yeah, seriously. You go ahead with them and I duck in here by myself, might be I never see you again." He pointed a thumb back along the trail they'd just hiked. "Who knows what's back there? I don't wanna break in a new group."

Bawdy nodded, he'd had that feeling too. Like Heraclitus' river, the trail always kept moving. Whenever you got off, the waters were entirely different when you returned. Except, it wasn't so much the actual, physical trail that changed as everything else. The people and weather and mood would have all tumbled merrily along without you. New people had caught up, and all the familiar folk had skipped ahead and disappeared, except for the harassing notes they left for you in the registers. No telling where or when or even *if* you might see them again.

"I could eat some serious pizza right now."

"Yeah?"

Bawdy patted his stomach. "And you probably don't remember this from Hot Springs, you know, since you were face down and snoring at the table, but I can really pour the beer down. After nine years of grad school, it's like I got a hollow leg. This could end up costing."

Coyote just grinned.

It was counter-intuitive, but Carvers Gap was actually up on top of Roan Mountain. There was a little paved road and a parking area with a nice permanent bathroom. An older couple in a pickup truck pulled alongside Skunkers just as he was crossing the road.

"You in a hurry, son?" the woman asked.

"No, ma'am. Katahdin by October if everything works out," Skunkers said.

"You wait around a bit, me and Jake, we got some food for ya."

Skunkers did more than wait around. He helped unload coolers and chairs, helped Jake unfold the folding tables and the portable grill and helped Janice set everything out before finally helping himself to the bounty that they had to offer. Homemade cookies, brownies and frosty-creamed cupcakes. Apples and oranges. Cold cokes and hot cocoa, corn chips, cookies, pretzels, and of course, the chili. Skunkers slurped up three bowls of the beef chili, each with a hunk of bread and butter and plenty of grated cheese.

When Flutterby arrived, Skunkers was wearing an apron, stirring the vats of chili and smiling ear-to-ear.

"Where's the other two at, Flubsy?"

"Ducked off to that hostel back before Roan."

"Suckers."

"Hope there's a lot of hikers coming behind you, honey," Janice said. "Jake made up sixteen gallons of chili. Skunkers here done his best to put a dent in it, but I reckon the poor boy's gonna burst if he don't get some help."

Flutterby introduced herself and tucked in to the food. Settled down into a folding chair with a bowl of vegetarian chili steaming on her lap. After the first delicious scoops, she asked Janice about herself.

Jake and Janice were both in their sixties. They'd met more than thirty years ago during a trail work party just north of Carvers Gap. New to the work, Jake had been assigned to Janice's crew. They spent three days roughing out new trail and stealing looks at each other. Now they lived together in Tennessee, not far from Fontana Dam, and for the last dozen years, they'd celebrated their anniversary by putting on a generous feed for thru-hikers.

🍁

It was the ol' poot & scoot pretty much the whole way down to Overmountain Shelter. Old Man Trouble had gotten talking with that Jake and somehow sucked down five bowls of chili. Old as he was, he should've known better.

That Jake made some good chili, though. Trouble just couldn't help himself.

So now, with his stomach bulging obscenely, he pooted and tooted and otherwise scooted along trail with a seemingly unending string of gassy explosions propelling him. Felt sorry for whoever was coming along behind.

❦ ❦ ❦

Register: Overmountain Shelter

5/6   Bartleby,
       I'm well beyond worry and beginning to fret.
       Can't imagine why you haven't caught up yet.
       Did you quit trail and slink home in shame?
       Get lost, get lazy or pull up lame?
       Or is it simply that: You would prefer not to?

       Your pal,
       Bawdy

❦ ❦ ❦

Poohbah kept talking about Overmountain Shelter like it was this awesome place. A must see. If anyone had asked, Bartleby would've admitted he was a little disappointed.

Turned out to be a huge, old red barn set at the top of a long grassy slope. 'Old' being the operative word.

Sure, it could easily fit a hundred thru-hikers, but the place was a rickety house of cards. Could come tumbling down any moment. The second story hayloft shook whenever anyone climbed the stairs. Where the board and batten siding wasn't missing, it had shrunk with time. Now it wasn't much tighter than the pickets on a fence. Just from a quick look, Bartleby could tell time and exposure hadn't been kind to the old barn's superstructure. The roof sagged and not one of the walls looked plumb.

Had he been carrying a tent, Bartleby would've happily slept outside.

Structural integrity or no, there was plenty of sleeping room for once; everyone could spread out, didn't have to sleep on top of each other in a great big puppy pile. This meant Lazy JoJo could surround herself with those mouse traps of hers and nobody had to worry about stepping on them in the middle of the night and losing a toe. Blitz could snore loud as he wanted and Bartleby could distance himself from it all.

Poohbah had also gone on about how Overmountain's privy had the best view on trail. This, it turned out, had been both the truth and a joke. The truth was that the privy was situated maybe fifty yards beyond the old barn and looked out on a beautiful valley meadow below. On a sunny late afternoon like this one, the pastoral view was breathtaking.

The joke being the privy itself. It was little more than a raised base with a broken seat hinge. Except for a few saplings whose leaves hadn't come in yet, nothing screened the privy from the barn. For one to use the privy, they would be, essentially, pooping in public. More than the surrounding countryside, this was what Poohbah had meant by the best view on trail.

Bartleby wasn't all that much bothered by the privy setup, but he imagined Pony wouldn't like it one bit.

Apparently, Overmountain was a popular hiker destination. A diverse crowd gathered there that night. Not just the thru-hiker (ir)regulars, but a handful of weekenders and a trio of men out for a longer section-hike. Quickshiver, Steakhouse Joe and Buffalo Nutz were back out for a two week reunion hike: Erwin to Damascus. Buffalo Nutz, his friends called him B-Nuts, was the group's elected spokesman. Came right up to Bartleby, made introductions and set to explaining how he and his compadres had met while thru-hiking in '02. Expected to reach Damascus in time for all the Trail Days ballyhoo. Actually used that word, ballyhoo.

If Bartleby wasn't lively or particularly willing, he was at least a captive audience. That, it turned out, was plenty fine with B-Nutz. He peppered Bartleby with nostalgic stories from the '02 trek: how he'd once gotten a hitch on a firetruck, about the time he woke up and mistakenly hiked south for six miles before running into fellow northbounders, or when a shelter mouse had snuck into his pack and birthed a litter there one night.

Even after the filtering process of those first few hundred miles on the AT, the lure of shelter living made for some strange bedfellows. More often than not, it was a unholy hodge-podge of individual foibles and personal idiosyncrasies.

Most mornings, Flutterby hummed as she swallowed her

coffee/oatmeal sludge and went about her chores. Couldn't stop if she tried. Luckily for those around her this was pleasingly melodic and hard to find fault with.

Coyote relentlessly looked for action or the next spot of trouble. When not playing cribbage with Skunkers, razzing Bawdy or sniffing around Flutterby, he was thinking up crazy bets and games to play.

Turned out, Bawdy had a little jester in him. He earned the spotlight with reenactments of old Monty Python bits, SNL skits and pitch-perfect impersonations of cartoon characters and fellow thru-hikers (his stiff-lipped rendition of Tommy Hawk brought Skunkers to tears). He had a superb memory for useless lyrics and throwaway jingles—could spit out theme songs to such classics as *Inspector Gadget*, *Hong Kong Phooey* and *The Jeffersons* without even trying.

Far as anyone could tell, it was physiologically impossible for Pork Chop to whisper. Didn't forget to, he simply couldn't. Wasn't built for it.

Lazy JoJo killed mice by the bucketful. Not a lot of things less pleasant than that sharp snap of a mousetrap in the middle of the night. And she didn't toss the broken little carcasses very far off into the woods. Come morning, sometimes people stepped on them.

Mad Chatter carried a handkerchief in his front pocket, used it to roto-root around in his nostrils with that unabashed enthusiasm only the oldest men can muster. When she wasn't tracking muddy prints across the shelter, Sweet Jane greatly enjoyed sniffing at crotches.

Socially speaking, Bartleby was a dud. He didn't talk enough, didn't add anything to ongoing conversations. He hovered on the fringes, smothering lively shelter banter like a wet blanket.

Pretty much everybody snored in their sleep except for Pony Express. He whimpered. It was *way* worse. He also spent long hours strategizing how best to avoid Jane's dogged attempts at friendship.

Regardless of how much she did or didn't drink beforehand, Giggles got up to pee six or seven times each night. And come morning, if there was any kind of line queued up outside the privy, she was begging her way to the front of it.

T-Ball spent hours picking at his feet. Draining blisters, cutting away dead skin and massaging the bottoms of sore feet with an old tennis ball he carried for just that purpose. Shaggy Bob chain smoked. Except for that first hour or so after showering, he stunk so strongly of stale smoke and sweat, it bordered on tangible. Squirtz endlessly described bowel movements and otherwise discussed his various digestive ailments ad nauseum.

Except when squabbling, Tortoise and Hairbrained bickered constantly.

Tommy Hawk arranged his sleeping area just so, setting out water, headlamp and toilet paper within easy reach. With that task completed, he whittled a point onto a stick and used it to clean the dirt from his boot lugs.

While waiting on dinner, Old Man Trouble sliced a clove of garlic so translucently thin, each piece melted on his tongue. Claimed it helped keep bugs away. After eating, he sometimes huffed tunelessly on a dented harmonica.

When Ella wasn't actively texting, talking or surfing the web, she was complaining about poor signal strength and lackluster battery life.

Before bedding down, Skunkers searched himself for ticks.

He liked to pinch any offenders between thumb and forefinger. Then he'd inch his lighter's flame closer and closer until the bloodsucker's legs shriveled up like the Wicked Witch's when Dorothy's house pancaked her.

Like it or not, shelters became the de facto home away from home for thru-hikers. And as with homes anywhere, hikers had little choice in the family with which they cohabited.

❧ ❧ ❧

The last mile or so to the top of Hump Mountain was grassy and open. Far over to the east, Coyote could see a handful of longhorn cattle, heads down and grazing. Run-off rain water had dug the trail into a rutted gully, knee-deep in places. This was because the trail didn't waste any time switchbacking or otherwise dawdling along the incline. It took a direct line to the summit. The climb was long and steep, but refreshing in its openness.

From Hump Mountain's rounded summit, the view was expansive. To the east and west, distant sprinklings of civilization were visible: water towers, church steeples and silver-topped farm silos. Back south, the way he'd just come, Coyote could see Little Hump Mountain and most of the lowland saddle connecting the summits.

Bawdy sat leaning against his pack, notebook in hand.

Coyote took a seat nearby, alternated sucking air and water. When his heart stopped threatening to explode, he started in on some pistachios.

"Think I can leave these shells here?"

"Shouldn't," Bawdy said.

"Pack in it, pack it out, huh?"

Bawdy nodded.

"Shit. Wasn't thinking about that when I bought them. Want some?"

"Sure."

"Actually, you can have them all if you'll carry the shells out."

"Pork 'em over. Did you see the register back at Overmountain?"

"Nope."

"Flubby left us a note. Guess they caught some awesome trail magic on Carvers Gap. Chili and fresh brownies and oranges and sodas."

"You kidding? That's a bad beat."

"Why? Sounded pretty good."

"Bad beat for *us*. I keep missing all the free food."

They watched a tiny figure hike down Little Hump's north slope and set off across the saddle towards Hump Mountain.

"Who is that?"

"Dunno. Moving fast though, huh?"

"Flying."

Turned out, the unidentified flying object was Ella. She reached the summit without visibly breaking a sweat. Instead of a backpack, she wore only a tiny stuff sack lashed over her shoulder with paracord.

"Jesus, she made that climb look easy."

"Don't make eye-contact. Maybe she'll keep going."

"That climb wasn't so bad," Ella trumpeted.

"Ignore her, she still might go away," Bawdy whispered.

"Where's your pack?" Coyote asked.

"T-Ball was meeting his girlfriend at Carvers Gap. They offered to take my backpack, stash it in the woods near Mountaineer Shelter."

"Seriously? When'd you see them?"

"I don't know—a few hours ago."

Coyote shook his head, "We musta just missed 'em."

"You guys should try slackpacking. You know, hiking without carrying your—"

"I know what slackpacking is," Bawdy sputtered irritably.

"Well, it's awesome," Ella sniffed. "Like someone turned off gravity."

With an insufferable little smile, she set off again, flouncing down trail feeling footloose and gravity free.

Register: Overmountain Shelter

5/9 I'm broke down, blistered and sunburnt, but happy to have finally tapped the brakes to let that big dumb Dane of a dog get a half-day ahead. She is <u>WAY</u> too friendly for this ex-postman.

Pony Express

"Okay, I'll bite," Bawdy said.

He was lying back on his sleeping bag with a book steepled on his chest. But instead of the book, he'd spent the last ten minutes reading the graffiti scrawled across the interior walls of Mountaineer Shelter.

Mostly the messages were of the "Andre the Giant has a Posse" or "Bad Johnny was NOT here '04, '05, '07" or "Honey Bear gots a Rumbley Tumbley" variety. But there was one name that kept coming up again and again.

Bob Peoples.

As in: "Bob Peoples Gave His Boots Blisters" and "Bob Peoples Hangs the Bears at Night" and Bawdy's favorite "The AT took six months off to hike Bob Peoples."

He couldn't take it anymore, "What the hell is a Bob Peoples?"

Some of the thru-hikers staying at Mountaineer Shelter were familiar, some weren't. One of the unfamiliar hikers, a puffy-haired guy going by Frizzly Adams, spoke up.

"He's this legendary wilderness dude. Like a caveman, almost, I think."

"Legendary like Paul Bunyan or legendary like Muir or Audubon?"

"He's real and I think he's still alive," Jersey George cut in. "So not like any of them. I heard he's old school special forces. This crazy-ass hardcore survivalist sniper guy. Just as soon kill ya, as not. Kinda like Bear Grylls, but you know, I don't think Bob ever got his own TV show."

"He's awesome," Squirtz said.

"Doesn't sound too awesome."

"See that episode when he climbed inside a dead camel carcass?"

Bawdy was confused, "I thought Peoples didn't have a show?"

"Bear Grylls. That guy will eat anything."

"We're not talking about Grylls. We're talking about Bob

Peoples."

"You see when he ate the bear poop?

"Yeah, and those raw goat testicles?"

❧

Now that his curiosity was up, Bawdy went looking for Old Man Trouble. He was tenting back along the ridge above the shelter.

"Hey, Trubs, what's the deal with this Bob Peoples dude?"

"Old cuss like me. Probably been around trail longer even. One of the best guys you'll ever meet—on or off the AT. You going into Kincora?"

"Dunno. Wasn't gonna. Should I?"

"Hell yes, you should. It's Bob Peoples' hiker hostel. Coming up in just fifteen miles. Take a left when you hit Dennis Cove Road. Be like a quarter mile up. You won't be sorry."

❧

Kincora was tucked around the back of Bob Peoples' house. The place was charming in an ivy-covered, rustic, rough-carpentry kind of way. Had a covered porch, multiple showers, free laundry, access to a full kitchen, a comfy little living room and something close to twenty bunks. Cost four dollars per night and that included a ride into the nearest shopping center.

It took Bawdy a bit to even figure out that the gimp-legged loudmouth collecting monies and otherwise ruling the roost wasn't Bob Peoples. It was Rhode Island Red, a longtime thru-hiker who didn't bother to hike so much anymore, but still haunted the AT for at least half the year. Apparently, Red had been hired on to help out during the busy season.

When Bawdy did locate him, Bob Peoples was not at all what he'd expected. The man was maybe in his late sixties with a head full of white hair and a small frame. He was soft-spoken and emanated a peaceful aura like a wise, old church mouse. Bob wasn't visible much, but when he was, he didn't talk at people, didn't give out unasked for advice, didn't hardly speak. Seemed content enough just to listen to hiker stories and nod along when appropriate.

Kincora was crowded full with a bunch of new faces.

There was the blotchy-skinned Calico Joe, Leaf-Stumper, Just Justine, the inscrutable Mr. Missouri, Billy Bonka (bumped his head four times in the course of fifteen minutes on the low rafters back at Spring Mountain Shelter), Galloping Goose, Disagreeable George (he was), Ixnay, Johnny Blue Jeans (who did not at all appreciate Bawdy calling him Johnny BJ), Optimus Grime, Kneejerk and a squishy fat guy going by the name of Gloop.

"Okay, let me guess," Bawdy said to him, "it's cuz you look like Augustus Gloop from *Charlie and the Chocolate Factory*? Am I good or am I good?"

"Nope, it's from—"

"*The Herculoids*! Gloop and Gleep. They were formless, fearless, buzzy blobs of intelligent protoplasm. I think Gloop was the big one. Come on—tell me that's it."

"I knocked over my water bottle at Hawk Mountain. The water made this gloopy-glugging noise as it spilled out."

"Really? That's it? You sure?"

"Yep."

"Huh."

"Sorry about him, Gloop, he spends way too much time in his head. I'm Flutterby."

"Flutterby, huh? Yeah, I heard about you. Thought you'd be taller. And blonder."

❦

"What's that mean? Blonder?"

"Dunno," Bawdy shrugged. He did know, but he wasn't saying anything.

He wandered a shopping cart through a grocery store. So far he'd grabbed a gallon of milk, half a gallon of orange juice, cream cheese, string cheese, cheddar cheese, cottage cheese and peanut butter. Fritos, bagels, tortillas, Swiss Cake Rolls, two pounds of peanut M&M's, carrots, tortellinis, mashed potatoes and a box of Apple Jacks.

Flutterby walked beside him, a shopping basket crooked in her arm.

"Seems like it's guy speak for something I don't know how to translate."

Bawdy was inspecting a jar of Marshmallow Fluff, "What'd'ya think?"

Flutterby wrinkled her nose and Bawdy returned it to the shelf.

Skunkers wheeled over holding two rotisserie chickens, "They only got three left, Bawds. Better hurry if you want one."

While Flutterby was distracted, Bawdy quick stuffed the Fluff into his cart.

She looked at all the food Bawdy and Skunkers had amassed

in their carts, "You guys know it's only another fifty miles of hiking to Damascus, right?'

Back at the hostel, Bawdy sat at the kitchen table. He poured his cook pot full of Apple Jacks. Skunkers joined him and proceeded to tear into those chickens like they'd personally wronged members of his family. He ripped limbs asunder, sucked marrow and sent hot grease spattering everywhere. Bawdy was hardly better, crunching away until there was nothing left but sugar-flavored, pastel colored milk. He drank this sugary slush down and helped himself to another pot full.

Register: Vandeventer Shelter

5/9   Got stopped by a bunch of picnickers at Watuga
       Lake. They stuffed me full of ribs, grilled corn and
       potato salad until I thought I was going to explode.
       Washed it all down with a cold glass of wine.
       Ya gotta luv' trail angels and their trail magic.
                                                    -Ella

Iron Mountain Shelter. Well past midnight.
HOO, HOO, TOO-HOO—HOO, HOO, TOO-HOO, OOO

Bartleby startled awake to the call of an owl. From the top of a nearby pine, the hoot echoed eerily across the dark woods, tumbling off into the night.

HOO, HOO, TOO-HOO—HOO, HOO, TOO-HOO, OOO

He listened with both eyes closed. Didn't need them open to recognize the imploring loneliness in the bird's cry. Bartleby was left wondering about his own dark solitude long after the owl had winged away over the forest.

🍁 🍁 🍁

Register: Double Springs Shelter

5/11 Less than twenty miles to Damascus. Rolled my ankle three times today. I am sore, swollen and hurtin' for certain. Looking forward to five days of R&R like a convict looks forward to parole.
And yes, I would know.

- Coyote "The Prison Rat" Slick

🍁

Flutterby disappeared off to her hammock and Skunkers into his tent. Coyote's ankle hurt and he'd crawled into his bag early to sleep/sulk. Ella commandeered the lion's share of the picnic table to shoot another video blog. After wandering back from filling his water bladder, Bawdy took a seat at the edge of the shelter and did his best to ignore Ella's lame journalistic endeavors.

Fireflies zipped through the near-dark. Bawdy sighed with boredom.

"Skunkers!"

No answer.

"Let's catch fireflies, Skunky."

No answer. Which was suspicious, because chasing after fireflies was right in Skunkers' wheelhouse. He usually spear-headed wackiness and he certainly didn't ignore invitations to it.

Bawdy ambled over to Skunkers' tent.

"You hear me?"

"Uh-huh."

"Wanna catch fireflies?"

"Uh-uh."

Bawdy peered into the tent, "What's going on in there? You okay?"

"Reading."

Bawdy looked around, like maybe the joke was somehow on him.

"Seriously. Everything alright, Skunks?"

Skunkers unzipped his tent flap, stuck his head out. "Yeah. Told you, I'm reading."

Bawdy put his hand out like 'hand it over, bucko.' As Skunkers did so, a blush started to show on his face.

Bawdy took one look, snorted, shook his head, "Where'd you get this?"

"In the last shelter. Thought, you know, I should maybe give it a try."

Bawdy squatted down close, "Listen Skunks. You know that books and reading are kinda my thing, right? And if you really want to start reading, I hope you'll believe me when I say I'm behind that, like, two hundred percent. Do you believe that?"

"Guess."

"Okay, good. How many novels have you read?"

"Counting that one?"

"What page are you on?"

"Three."

"Well for now, let's say *not* counting this one."

"None, I guess."

"Okay. So as I see it, it's like you're a promising rookie, right? And I'm the seasoned old pro who's seen it all before. You with me?

"Uh-huh."

"So as the old pro, I'd like to suggest you not start your reading career with *The Sound and The Fury*."

"Heard you talk about this dude."

"Fuck Faulkner and his fucking fury. This book gives me a migraine. You wanna read a book, I got the perfect one. Hold on."

Bawdy hustled to the shelter and returned clutching both halves of *Slaughterhouse-Five*. "Give this bad boy a try. It's about World War II and it's actually accessible."

"Yeah?"

"It's got drawings of buttholes and everything. You're gonna love it, dude."

❦ ❦ ❦

After the first couple hundred miles, Flutterby's body found its comfort zone in a short-strided, fast-legged pace that let her eat up miles without too much effort. After an unfortunate series of stubbed toes resulted in the loss of two toenails, she kept a wary eye peeled for rocks and roots lurking with ill intentions.

Coyote's heels didn't touch ground more than once or twice every mile. He took lots and lots of mincing fast steps. His eyes were constantly scanning ahead, reading the ground and figuring where to step next.

Despite steady weight loss, Bawdy still waddled along with his feet splayed outward like some fat-bottomed woodchuck. On steep downhill slopes, he led with his right foot in a step-stop, step-stop style that wasn't very fast or efficient, but gave him plenty of control.

Skunkers' long loping strides looked slow and leisurely, but somehow he moved faster than pretty much anyone else out there.

Bartleby trudged along like he was dragging a ball and chain behind each leg.

There was nothing noteworthy about the mechanics of Ella's stride, except for the aggressiveness with which she stepped. Up, down, straightaway, it didn't matter—she tromped with a certitude and conviction, a nothing-is-gonna-stop-me-from-hiking-this-trail attitude that stood her in good stead right up until she gave herself shin splints.

Old Man Trouble barely lifted his feet off the ground. He scuffled along, leaving a puffy string of dust clouds in his wake.

Almost without exception, and with surprising disregard for the terrain, Tommy Hawk's strides were improbably uniform in length and velocity.

The symmetry of Pony Express' gait was all off. His left leg led, fast and light, and the right leg followed with a slower, hitched step. Like maybe he could still feel the weight of a phantom mail bag swinging at his side.

Register: Abingdon Gap Shelter

5/7   Miracles abound
        on the road to Damascus.
        Trail angel food cake.
                            High-Ku

Oddly enough, Bawdy and Flutterby heard Virginia's border well before they ever saw it. It was getting on to midafternoon. They had something like four miles still to go into Damascus.

It was the damnedest thing. Bawdy was hiking along, drafting close behind Flutterby. They'd talked themselves out an hour earlier, so had been progressing steadily in a comfortable silence. Then out of nowhere, Bawdy started to hear music. At first, it was soft little snatches, sometimes no more than a single note.

"You hear something?"

Flutterby kept on trucking, "Besides you wheezing?"

"What'd'ya want me to do? I got allergies. Stop for a sec, Flubby."

They stopped and listened. Couldn't hear anything but their own breathing.

"Huh. Guess I'm making things up. Sorry."

Started hiking again. The music was still sporadic, but growing noticeably stronger.

"I hear it now," she said. "Gotta be music, right?"

"Sure sounds like it."

They finally came up on a wooden sign post demarking the Tennessee/Virginia state line. Incongruously, there was also a tiny woman sitting there on a portable amp, plucking out a soulful lament on an Irish harp. Bawdy vaguely recognized her from Neels Gap. It was the thru-hiking harpist chick, Finger Pickin' Good. She must've yellow-blazed ahead, there was no way she hiked past Bawdy without him seeing her or that harp of hers.

The instrument's case was set out and open in front of her. Visible there amongst a pathetic smattering of coins and dirty dollar bills was a single crisp hundo.

Even before they'd come to a complete stop, Finger Pickin' struck up a new tune.

Took Bawdy about two chords to recognize it as the opening gambit of *The Imperial March*. Darth Vader's theme song.

He shook his head, grinned ruefully. "Coyote paid you to play this for me?"

Finger Pickin' nodded, shrugged and continued plucking.

"How'd you know I was the one to play it for?"

"You match his description."

"Let's hear it."

The little harpist winced, "He said I should play it for the next four-eyed, food-stained, mullet-headed butterball to come waddling through."

❧ ❧ ❧

From the border, the trail sloped three-point-seven miles down into Damascus, Virginia. It was early evening; Bartleby's best guess put it just before six. Once into the town proper, the AT meandered along a side road, past neat homes and a town green before turning right up Laurel Avenue.

❧

Squatting right there on Laurel, Quincey's Pizza served up hot food and cold beer.

Inside the pizzeria, Bawdy was sitting at a table, surrounded by the regular suspects. They ordered too many pitchers and not enough pizzas. While they consumed the former and waited on the later, Bawdy happened to catch a glimpse of something outside on the street. Did a double-take. Took off his glasses, rubbed his eyes. Then he dashed out of the restaurant without a word. When he came back a minute later, he was pulling another hiker by the shoulder strap.

"There's no way you're not having a beer with us, so stop dragging ass," Bawdy said. He wrangled another chair for the table before introducing Bartleby around.

"So I think you know Coyote, and this crusty bastard is Old Man Trouble. And Skunkers here, he's our resident rube. He'll believe absolutely anything you tell him."

"That's not—"

"You got some shit on your shirt," Coyote said, pointed at an imaginary spot on Skunkers' chest.

"What? Where?" When Skunkers looked down, Coyote chucked him on the chin.

"And that's Flutterby—"

"You look familiar," Bartleby said.

"I better. You gave me my name back on the stairs at Amicalola."

Bawdy pushed Bartleby down into a chair.

"Fuckin' A, people, this is the dude I been tellin' you about. Probably the only guy in history out hiking the AT against his will."

"I didn't hear nuttin' about this," Skunkers said.

"Yeah, you did," Coyote said. "Remember the guy who wore steel-toed boots and blue jeans, carried like twenty pounds of canned food?"

"Yeah?"

"This is *that* guy."

"But hiking against his will?"

They all looked to Bartleby.

He paused, blinked, "My wife pushed me outta the car. Said I needed a new perspective."

Silence.

"That's broke-dick," Skunkers finally said.

"That's some wife," Trouble offered. "I gotta spend a full year kissing my wife's bony old ass before she lets me step one foot into the woods."

"So what happened? I lost you like five weeks ago at Neels Gap. Figured you musta quit."

"Didn't quit."

"No shit ya didn't quit! But how are ya? How's it been?"

Bartleby shrugged, "Alright. You get a new shirt?"

Coyote hooted and bumped knucks with Skunkers. "Sloppy Joe here decided to wear one of his meals 'stead a eat it. Had this big ol' grease stain on his stomach."

Ignoring Coyote, Bawdy filled a pint glass from one of the pitchers, put it in front of Bartleby. "Goddamned, Bartleby— it's good to see you, even if you are a mopey-ass Eeyore. Get that waitress, Coyote. We're gonna see what it takes to loosen this guy's tongue."

❧

"You take any zeros?

"Uh-uh."

"Spend a night in Erwin?"

"Showered there."

"Did you have some fun in Hot Springs? We raised some Cain, didn't we Skunks?"

"You betcha, Bawds."

When Bartleby didn't offer up any story of his own, Bawdy kept on, "You go into Gatlinburg or Greasy Creek? Or how about Kincora—that place was sweet, right?"

"What's Kincora?"

"What the hell have you been doing back there?"

Bawdy kept topping off his beer, so Bartleby had no idea how much he'd drunk. He knew he was well on his way, though, because his fingers weren't listening so well anymore, and they were always the first to go. Angie used to say he got fumbly-fingered. They'd be out with friends, having a nice time, and then he'd go and drop a beer right out of his hand. Was like his fingers called a time-out without telling the rest of him. Sometimes the bottle smashed, made a huge mess. Usually it didn't.

Christ, did he miss Angie.

He didn't know what he'd been doing back there. Nothing but walking, really. Thinking back now on the past weeks, very little stood out. Mostly, he slugged along with his head down. Except for that hour up on Max Patch. Couldn't guess why, but he'd felt something up there. Awake, alive or like the power had been switched back on. It was the best he'd felt in a thousand years. Maybe Angie'd been right, maybe this hike could help make him better. So far at least, it'd been better for him than pretty much anything else.

He fumbled for his wallet, slowly counted his cash, "Looks like I got two-hundred thirty-one dollars left. Is that gonna be enough, Bawdy?"

"For the weekend?"

"To get me to Maine."

"Not likely, bro. Hell, you might not get you out of Damascus on two hundred. As Skunkers says, we're got some serious R&R coming our way these next five days."

❦

The crowd inside Quincey's grew significantly over the next hour. There was somewhere in the neighborhood of fifty thru-hikers drinking, socializing and generally applauding themselves for having made it into Virginia.

"Trail Days," Skunkers bellowed through mega-phoned hands.

The hodge-podge of hikers responded back with raised drinks and a raucous cheer.

When Bartleby returned from the men's room, his seat was occupied. So he started skulking around the room, lurking on the periphery of conversations. Made sure to hold his beer with both hands.

Ended up standing near Giggles and Pork Chop. She'd bought a wall map at the outfitter. It was a foot wide and all of four feet tall. They were holding it between them and studying it. Bartleby couldn't help but to lean in for a close look.

"This the trail?"

"Uh-huh."

"Where we at?"

"Right here," Giggles pointed a finger at Virginia's southern border, maybe a hand's length from the map's bottom edge.

"That all we did? Doesn't look like so much."

"That's cuz Springer to Damascus is only like four hundred and fifty miles," Pork Chop said.

"Only four-fifty," Bartleby echoed.

"About another seventeen hundred miles to go," Giggles said. "Or put it this way. They say it's about five million steps from Springer to Katahdin and we just did about a million of those. Still got like four million steps to go. Wild, huh?"

Wild wasn't the word Bartleby would've used. He might've used shocking or discouraging or maybe epic. The sheer enormity of the task looming before him began to sink in.

After spending most of six weeks on trail, he wasn't even a quarter way finished. But he was down to about a quarter of the money he'd started with. The math was not looking good at all.

Bartleby looked for Bawdy. Found him talking to a large-framed man with a gnarly black beard.

"Bartleby, this is Papa Bear. He hiked last year. Drove down from Vermont just for Trail Days."

Papa Bear smiled down, "How's your hike going so far?" Against the black backdrop of thick beard, Papa Bear's teeth shone white as a cluster of wishing stars.

"Well, Papa Bear," Bartleby said, "I'm glad you asked. How's it going? Let's see. Looks like I've walked most, but not quite all of the infection out of my horribly blistered feet. My knees haven't stopped hurting for one single minute since somewhere around Hot Springs. My gear's for shit and I'm drinking the last of my money right now, which, you probably know, really isn't very good timing considering we've got seventeen hundred miles left to Katahdin.

"What's worse, I've somehow become such a numb schlump of a man that my wife, a woman who I would classify as generally uncomfortable behind the wheel of a car, felt compelled to drive me down from Connecticut and kick me out at Amicalola. All on the remote chance that hiking the AT was gonna somehow save me, and by extension, her and us and our kids. Which is, I gotta say, quite a bit to ask from a simple walk in the woods. And you know what? I spent that whole drive begging her to turn around, just let me go home. But that's just *my* take on these first four-hundred fifty miles. Bawdy's perspective could be entirely different."

It was in the first moments after this unplanned and uncensored confession that Bartleby's fingers gave up all pretense of holding his beer. The pint glass slipped from his hand and shattered on the tile floor. Bits of glass and beer foam speckled his bare legs.

As crowds invariably do whenever a plate is dropped or glassware shatters, the Quincey's crowd went momentarily silent.

This silence was filled by a cavernous guffaw. Papa Bear's

laughter was deep and bassy. It was something you felt as much as heard, like a heavy truck rumbling by outside.

He threw a hairy paw over Bartleby's shoulder, "Maybe you could use a ride home, friend. Come Monday morning, I'm heading north. Happy to have some good company."

"First of all," Bartleby said, his head already shaking no, "and I think Bawdy here would have to agree, I'm not any kind of good company. You'd be regretting my presence in the first hour. It's a generous offer, thoughtful and all that, but honestly, going home is not even close to what I need to do right now. You see me here, talking like this? I bet I haven't talked this much in two years. And I know I haven't *felt* this worked up. Haven't felt anything. Makes me think that maybe this Appalachian Trail is, well, it's gotten into my blood now. So what I *need* to do is buck up, stick it out and see."

"Sounds like ya gotta keep on keepin' on."

"Yes sir," Bartleby cymballed his hands together, "that's just what I gotta do."

END BOOK ONE

Made in the USA
San Bernardino, CA
11 April 2015